Chicken Now

Jean Paré

www.companyscoming.com
visit our ↖website

Front Cover

1. Citrus Spice Chicken, page 44

Props courtesy of: Casa Bugatti
Cherison Enterprises Inc.
The Bay

Back Cover

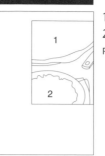

1. Chicken Paella, page 82
2. Coconut Curry Casserole, page 60

Props courtesy of: Browne & Company

We gratefully acknowledge the following suppliers for their generous support of our Test and Photography Kitchens:

Broil King Barbecues   *Hamilton Beach® Canada*   *Proctor Silex® Canada*
Corelle®   *Lagostina®*   *Tupperware®*

Chicken Now

Second Printing May 2007

Library and Archives Canada Cataloguing in Publication
Paré, Jean, date
Chicken now / Jean Paré.
(Original series)
Includes index.
ISBN 978-1-897069-24-0
1. Cookery (Chicken). 2. Cookery (Turkey). I. Title.
II. Series: Paré, Jean, 1927- . Original series.
TX750.5.C45P373 2007   641.6′65   C2006-906131-9

Published by
Company's Coming Publishing Limited
2311 – 96 Street
Edmonton, Alberta, Canada T6N 1G3
Tel: 780-450-6223   Fax: 780-450-1857
www.companyscoming.com

Company's Coming is a registered trademark owned by
Company's Coming Publishing Limited

We acknowledge the financial support of the Government of Canada through the
Book Publishing Industry Development Program (BPIDP) for our publishing activities.

Printed in Canada

Cooking tonight?

A selection of
feature recipes
is only a
click away—
absolutely **FREE!**

Visit us at

www.companyscoming.com

Company's Coming Cookbooks

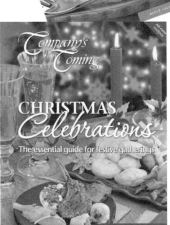

Original Series

- Softcover, 160 pages
- 6" x 9" (15 cm x 23 cm) format
- Lay-flat plastic comb binding
- Full-colour photos
- Nutrition information

Lifestyle Series

- Softcover, 160 pages
- 8" x 10" (20 cm x 25 cm) format
- Paperback
- Full-colour photos
- Nutrition information

Most Loved Recipe Collection

- Hardcover, 128 pages
- 8 3/4" x 8 3/4" (22 cm x 22 cm) format
- Durable sewn binding
- Full-colour throughout
- Nutrition information

Special Occasion Series

- Hardcover & softcover
- 8 1/2" x 11" (22 cm x 28 cm) format
- Durable sewn binding
- Full-colour throughout
- Nutrition information

See page 157 for more cookbooks.
For a complete listing, visit
www.companyscoming.com

Table of Contents

The Company's Coming Story

Jean Paré (pronounced "jeen PAIR-ee") grew up understanding that the combination of family, friends and home cooking is the best recipe for a good life. From her mother, she learned to appreciate good cooking, while her father praised even her earliest attempts in the kitchen. When Jean left home, she took with her a love of cooking, many family recipes and an intriguing desire to read cookbooks as if they were novels!

"never share a recipe you wouldn't use yourself"

In 1963, when her four children had all reached school age, Jean volunteered to cater the 50th Anniversary of the Vermilion School of Agriculture, now Lakeland College, in Alberta, Canada. Working out of her home, Jean prepared a dinner for more than 1,000 people, which launched a flourishing catering operation that continued for over 18 years. During that time, she had countless opportunities to test new ideas with immediate feedback—resulting in empty plates and contented customers! Whether preparing cocktail sandwiches for a house party or serving a hot meal for 1,500 people, Jean Paré earned a reputation for good food, courteous service and reasonable prices.

As requests for her recipes mounted, Jean was often asked the question, "Why don't you write a cookbook?" Jean responded by teaming up with her son, Grant Lovig, in the fall of 1980 to form Company's Coming Publishing Limited. The publication of *150 Delicious Squares* on April 14, 1981 marked the debut of what would soon become one of the world's most popular cookbook series.

The company has grown since those early days when Jean worked from a spare bedroom in her home. Today, she continues to write recipes while working closely with the staff of the Recipe Factory, as the Company's Coming test kitchen is affectionately known. There she fills the role of mentor, assisting with the development of recipes people most want to use for everyday cooking and easy entertaining. Every Company's Coming recipe is *kitchen-tested* before it's approved for publication.

Jean's daughter, Gail Lovig, is responsible for marketing and distribution, leading a team that includes sales personnel located in major cities across Canada. In addition, Company's Coming cookbooks are published and distributed under licence in the United States, Australia and other world markets. Bestsellers many times over in English, Company's Coming cookbooks have also been published in French and Spanish.

Familiar and trusted in home kitchens around the world, Company's Coming cookbooks are offered in a variety of formats. Highly regarded as kitchen workbooks, the softcover Original Series, with its lay-flat plastic comb binding, is still a favourite among readers.

Jean Paré's approach to cooking has always called for *quick and easy recipes* using *everyday ingredients.* That view has served her well. The recipient of many awards, including the Queen Elizabeth Golden Jubilee medal, Jean was appointed a Member of the Order of Canada, her country's highest lifetime achievement honour.

Jean continues to gain new supporters by adhering to what she calls The Golden Rule of Cooking: *"Never share a recipe you wouldn't use yourself."* It's an approach that works— *millions of times over!*

Foreword

Why did the chicken cross the road? To get away from all the people who've discovered what a delicious, healthy and versatile meal it makes!

It seems we can't get enough chicken. These days the average Canadian eats about 67 pounds (30.5 kg) a year, up by more than 30 per cent in the last decade. That's not chicken feed!

And we've all become aware of the nutritional value of this great protein source. High in B vitamins and niacin, chicken is a terrific addition to a balanced diet. White meat is a wonderful low-fat choice, especially once the skin is removed, while the dark meat is high in iron and zinc.

It's easy to see why chicken is so popular when you're feeling peckish. You can dress it up for company or dress it down for fast family meals. You can choose between dark or white meat, or cook it whole, ground or in separate pieces—and it's equally delicious served hot or cold.

To reflect chicken's unrelenting popularity, we've put together this second cookbook on the subject, chock full of all-new recipes. *Chicken Now* features this much beloved meat in appetizers, soups, salads and entrees.

We've included updates of old favourites, such as Chicken Sloppy Joes and Sunday Fried Chicken. But we hope you won't chicken out from trying such tasty new flavour combinations as our fragrant Coconut Curry Rice Casserole or the chocolatey(!) Chicken Aztec.

You'll also want to check out our special turkey chapter, featuring many of the new cuts on the market, as well as fresh ideas for gobbling up leftovers. We've even included a flock of tips on shopping, storing, cooking and carving your poultry, as well as a number of safety suggestions.

Putting together a meal you can crow about is so easy when you pick up *Chicken Now!*

Jean Paré

Nutrition Information Guidelines

Each recipe is analyzed using the most current version of the Canadian Nutrient File from Health Canada, which is based on the United States Department of Agriculture (USDA) Nutrient Database.

- If more than one ingredient is listed (such as "butter or hard margarine"), or if a range is given (1 – 2 tsp., 5 – 10 mL), only the first ingredient or first amount is analyzed.

- For meat, poultry and fish, the serving size per person is based on the recommended 4 oz. (113 g) uncooked weight (without bone), which is 2 – 3 oz. (57 – 85 g) cooked weight (without bone)—approximately the size of a deck of playing cards.

- Milk used is 1% M.F. (milk fat), unless otherwise stated.

- Cooking oil used is canola oil, unless otherwise stated.

- Ingredients indicating "sprinkle," "optional," or "for garnish" are not included in the nutrition information.

- The fat in recipes and combination foods can vary greatly depending on the sources and types of fats used in each specific ingredient. For these reasons, the amount of saturated, monounsaturated and polyunsaturated fats may not add up to the total fat content.

Vera C. Mazurak, Ph.D.
Nutritionist

All about chicken...and a little about turkey, too!

Whether they're fryers or roasters, air-chilled or pre-stuffed, there are so many chicken options in the market today that it's easy to become overwhelmed. And what about all the food safety rules? The following guide will help you make the most of this versatile meal option, from purchasing to putting away the leftovers.

Safety First
Smart shopping

- Choose cold, tightly-wrapped packages with no holes or tears.
- Check labels for "best before" dates.
- Pick up your poultry items just before you head to the checkout and get them home within 2 hours (1 hour if it's hot outside).
- Tuck packages of poultry into produce bags so they don't leak on other groceries.

Fridge and freezer fundamentals

- Immediately refrigerate or freeze poultry. Store whole poultry and poultry parts in the fridge for up to 2 days, and ground chicken for no more than 24 hours. Place the poultry on a plate or tray on the bottom shelf to prevent juices from contaminating other foods.
- To freeze, wrap fresh poultry packages with airtight heavy-duty foil, freezer wrap or freezer paper, or place the contents in freezer bags. Poultry pieces may be frozen for 6 to 9 months.
- Frozen whole poultry purchased in tightly wrapped, heavy-duty plastic vacuum bags may be frozen as is for up to 1 year and do not need to be rewrapped.

Defrosting directions (or defrosting de poultry)

NEVER defrost poultry at room temperature. Use the following methods and tips:

- Refrigerator Method (recommended): Good for poultry pieces and whole poultry. Place poultry on a tray in the fridge to prevent thawing juices from cross-contaminating other items and allow 5 hours per pound (10 hours per kilogram).

- Cold Water Method: Suitable for whole poultry purchased frozen in tightly wrapped, heavy-duty plastic. Submerge it in its original wrappings in cold water. Change the water every 30 minutes. 1 hour per pound (2 hours per kilogram) to defrost.

- Microwave Method: If using the microwave for poultry pieces, remove the pieces closest to the edge of the plate as they thaw, and cook immediately after defrosting.

- Make sure a whole bird is completely thawed before cooking or else frozen meat closest to the bone will be undercooked, dramatically affecting the cooking time.

- Frozen poultry purchased pre-stuffed is designed to be cooked frozen. Do not thaw before cooking.

Cooking criteria

- Do NOT wash raw poultry before cooking as this can spread bacteria to kitchen surfaces.

- Use paper towels, not cloth, to wipe up any spilled poultry juices.

- Don't use the same utensils or dishes when handling raw and then cooked poultry.

- Wash hands, utensils and work surfaces with hot water and soap after handling or preparing poultry. To sanitize, mix 1 tsp. (5 mL) bleach with 3 cups (750 mL) water for use on drains, cutting boards, taps and fridge door handles.

- Marinate poultry in the refrigerator for up to 2 days, but never at room temperature.

- Make sure stuffing is completely cooled before inserting into the cavity.

- Stuff a whole bird JUST before cooking. Stuff no more than 2/3 full as the stuffing will expand during cooking.

- When basting, brush sauce on cooked surfaces only. Don't use a brush that has previously been in contact with raw poultry.

- Leftover marinade must be boiled 5 to 7 minutes before basting or dipping. Better yet, set aside part of the marinade before you marinate. Don't reuse marinades.

- Always cook poultry until done. Partial cooking can encourage bacterial growth.

9

Temperature tips

- The Canadian Partnership for Consumer Food Safety Education recommends using a digital instant-read thermometer or thermometer fork that gives a temperature reading, and not just a doneness range, to test for accurate, safe internal temperatures. Wash the device in hot, soapy water after use.
- To check that your thermometer is accurate, place it in boiling water and see if it reaches 212°F (100°C).
- Insert the thermometer into the thickest part of the food, away from bone, fat or gristle, and hold it there for at least 30 seconds.

- How to insert the thermometer:
  - **In poultry pieces:** remove the pieces from heat and insert thermometer horizontally into the centre of the thickest part, for a depth of at least 1 1/2 inches (4 cm).
  - **In whole chicken:** insert the thermometer stem into the thickest end of the breast, near the wing, so the stem points toward the drumstick.
  - **In whole turkey:** insert the thermometer into the thickest part of the inner thigh.

Temperature rules for safe doneness (Canadian industry standards)

Ground chicken or turkey	175°F	(80°C)
Chicken or turkey pieces	170°F	(77°C)
Whole chicken (without stuffing)	180°F	(82°C)
Whole stuffed chicken (temperature measured in meat)	180°F	(82°C)
Whole turkey (without stuffing)	165°F	(74°C)
Whole stuffed turkey (temperature measured in meat)	180°F	(82°C)
Stuffing cooked in poultry	165°F	(74°C)

Leftover laws

- Refrigerate leftovers within 2 hours, or 1 hour if the room temperature is more than 90°F (32°C).
- Remove any meat from the carcass immediately after the first meal and store in the refrigerator in shallow containers so it can cool quickly.

- Boil the carcass for soup within 3 days, or freeze for up to 3 months.
- Use refrigerated poultry and stuffing within 3 days, and gravy within 1 to 2 days.
- Cooked poultry may be frozen for up to 3 months.

Tricky terms

Types of chicken

The different labels on whole chickens relate to their size:

- A **broiler** or **fryer** is a young chicken weighing 1.5 to 3.86 pounds (700 g to 1.75 kg).
- A **roaster** weighs more than 3.86 pounds (1.75 kg).
- A **stewing hen** is an older hen of about 5.5 pounds (2.5 kg), best suited for moist cooking methods such as braising and stewing.

Air-chilled vs. water-chilled

Both methods refer to the way poultry is cooled.

- **Air-chilling** is the newer method. Chicken and turkey are placed on conveyor belts and cooling fans quickly reduce their temperature to less than 39.2°F (4°C).
- **Water- or immersion-chilling** is the older method. The meat is submerged in cold water to reduce the temperature. Federal regulations restrict the increase of body weight through this process to a maximum of 8 per cent.

Generally, if you don't see the label "air-chilled," it means that the poultry product has been water-chilled.

Substitution strategies

If a recipe calls for chicken breasts and your freezer's full of thighs, you can substitute, but keep the following in mind:

- If it calls for a bone-in part, use a bone-in equivalent of the same weight.
- If it calls for a boneless part, use a boneless equivalent of the same weight.
- Remember that white meat cooks more quickly than dark meat. Adjust cooking times accordingly.

Turkey roasting times

There are general guidelines for how long turkeys of certain weights should be cooked, but it is important to know that a **turkey is only truly cooked when it reaches its safe internal temperature**. Cooking times can vary based on how many times the oven door is opened, the size of the oven, whether the oven is a convection oven…the list goes on and on! So, although the following chart can be used as a guideline, it won't tell you when your turkey is done—you must use a meat thermometer for that.

size	without stuffing	with stuffing
6 – 8 lbs (3 – 3.5 kg)	2 ½ – 2 ¾ hours	3 – 3 ¼ hours
8 – 10 lbs (3.5 – 4.5 kg)	2 ¾ – 3 hours	3 ¼ – 3 ½ hours
10 – 12 lbs (4.5 – 5.5 kg)	3 – 3 ¼ hours	3 ½ – 3 ¾ hours
12 – 16 lbs (5.5 – 7 kg)	3 ¼ – 3 ½ hours	3 ¾ – 4 hours
16 – 22 lbs (7 – 10 kg)	3 ½ – 4 hours	4 – 4 ½ hours

* based on a pre-heated 325°F (160°C) standard oven

Carving cues

Depending on your preference, carving can take place in the kitchen or at the table:

For carving at the table

1. Let the whole bird sit for 20 minutes to allow the juices to distribute properly. If you begin right away, the juices will run out and you'll be left with dry meat.

2. Arrange the bird, breast-side up and drumsticks pointed toward you, on a warmed platter.

3. If the drumsticks are tied together, cut off the string.

4. Remove all the stuffing from the bird and place in a separate dish.

5. Insert a fork into a thigh. Place a sharp knife between the thigh and the body of the bird and cut through the skin to the joint. Use the point of the knife to work through the joint.

6. Separate the thigh and drumstick at the joint.

7. With the fork, pull the wing away from the shoulder joint and cut at the joint.

8. Make a long, horizontal cut above the wing joint into the body frame through the breast. This is your base cut.

9. About halfway up the breast, slice straight down with an even stroke. The slice will fall free when the knife reaches the base cut.

10. Continue to slice breast meat, starting the cut a bit higher for each slice.

11. Repeat steps 5 to 10 on the other side.

For carving in the kitchen

Repeat steps 1- 8, but place all the carved pieces on a heated platter.

9. Slice the whole piece of breast meat from the bird by making a slice down the centre of the bird, on one side of the breast bone.

10. Place the breast meat, skin-side up, on a carving board and cut thin slices across the grain. Place on the heated platter.

11. Repeat steps 5 to 10 on the other side.

Chicken Salad Shells

Almost too cute for words, these tiny chicken salad servings
are all dolled up in crunchy, edible shells. Delicious!

Mayonnaise	2 tbsp.	30 mL
Lime juice	1 tbsp.	15 mL
Sweet chili sauce	1 tbsp.	15 mL
Soy sauce	2 tsp.	10 mL
Diced cooked chicken (see Tip, on page 26)	1 1/4 cups	300 mL
Finely chopped celery	1/4 cup	60 mL
Finely chopped red pepper	1/4 cup	60 mL
Finely sliced green onion	3 tbsp.	50 mL
Pepper	1/4 tsp.	1 mL
Packages of Siljan mini croustade shells (24 per package), see Note	2	2
Sesame seeds, toasted (see Tip)	2 tsp.	10 mL

Combine first 4 ingredients in medium bowl.

Add next 5 ingredients. Stir.

Spoon chicken mixture into croustade shells.

Sprinkle with sesame seeds. Serve immediately. Makes 48 salad shells.

1 salad shell: 19 Calories; 1.1 g Total Fat (0.4 g Mono, 0.2 g Poly, 0.2 g Sat); 4 mg Cholesterol;
1 g Carbohydrate; trace Fibre; 1 g Protein; 48 mg Sodium

Pictured on page 17.

Note: Croustade shells can generally be found in either the deli, cracker or imported section of your grocery store.

tip When toasting nuts, seeds or coconut, cooking times will vary for each different ingredient—so never toast them together. For small amounts, place ingredient in an ungreased shallow frying pan. Heat on medium for 3 to 5 minutes, stirring often, until golden. For larger amounts, spread ingredient evenly in an ungreased shallow pan. Bake in a 350°F (175°C) oven for 5 to 10 minutes, stirring or shaking often, until golden.

Chicken Spinach Rolls

Let the good times roll! These pretty white and green spirals
are a terrific choice for a dinner party. For even more colour,
use tomato or spinach tortillas. Serve hot or cold.

Cooking oil	1 tsp.	5 mL
Lean ground chicken	1/2 lb.	225 g
Finely chopped onion	2 tbsp.	30 mL
Salt	1/4 tsp.	1 mL
Pepper	1/8 tsp.	0.5 mL
Ground nutmeg	1/8 tsp.	0.5 mL
Box of frozen chopped spinach, thawed and squeezed dry	10 oz.	300 g
Cream cheese, softened and cut up	4 oz.	113 g
Finely chopped dried cranberries	1/4 cup	60 mL
Finely chopped pecans	2 tbsp.	30 mL
Flour tortillas (9 inch, 22 cm, diameter)	4	4

Heat cooking oil in medium frying pan on medium. Add next 5 ingredients. Scramble-fry for about 5 minutes until chicken is no longer pink and any liquid has evaporated.

Add spinach. Heat and stir until just combined. Transfer to medium bowl.

Add next 3 ingredients. Stir well.

Spread chicken mixture evenly on each tortilla, almost to edge. Roll up tightly, jelly-roll style. Trim ends. Cut each roll diagonally into 8 slices. Makes 32 slices.

1 slice: 64 Calories; 3.4 g Total Fat (0.6 g Mono, 0.3 g Poly, 1.0 g Sat); 4 mg Cholesterol; 6 g Carbohydrate; 1 g Fibre; 3 g Protein; 100 mg Sodium

Paré Pointer
She left her job due to illness. The boss was sick of her.

Onion Apple Phyllo Rolls

These appies are chic and dashing, tantalizing and tempting.

Butter (or hard margarine)	2 tbsp.	30 mL
Chopped onion	2 cups	500 mL
Grated peeled cooking apple (such as McIntosh)	1 cup	250 mL
Lean ground chicken	1/2 lb.	225 g
Grated Gruyère cheese	2/3 cup	150 mL
Chopped fresh thyme (or 1/2 tsp., 2 mL, dried)	2 tsp.	10 mL
Salt	1/2 tsp.	2 mL
Pepper	1/4 tsp.	1 mL
Phyllo pastry sheets, thawed according to package directions	6	6
Butter (or hard margarine), melted	1/3 cup	75 mL

Melt first amount of butter in large frying pan on medium. Add onion. Cook for 5 to 10 minutes, stirring often, until softened.

Add apple. Stir. Reduce heat to medium-low. Cook for about 20 minutes, stirring occasionally, until onion is very soft and golden. Transfer to medium bowl. Cool for 10 minutes.

Add next 5 ingredients. Mix well.

Lay pastry sheets on top of each other. Cut sheets in half crosswise, making 12 sheets. Place 1 sheet on work surface with long side closest to you. Cover remaining sheets with damp towel to prevent drying.

Brush sheet with melted butter. Cut sheet in half crosswise. Place about 1 tbsp. (15 mL) chicken mixture on lowest end of 1 half of sheet, about 1 inch from edge. Fold bottom edge of sheet over chicken mixture. Fold in sides. Roll up from bottom to enclose filling. Place seam-side down on greased baking sheet with sides. Cover with separate damp towel. Repeat with remaining pastry sheets and chicken mixture. Brush tops of rolls with any remaining butter. Bake in 400°F (205°C) oven for about 15 minutes until pastry is golden, chicken is no longer pink and internal temperature reaches 175°F (80°C). Makes 24 rolls.

1 roll: 82 Calories; 5.9 g Total Fat (1.3 g Mono, 0.2 g Poly, 2.7 g Sat); 12 mg Cholesterol; 4 g Carbohydrate; trace Fibre; 3 g Protein; 111 mg Sodium

Pictured on page 17.

Nutty Crunch Drumettes

Everyone will go nuts for these crisp and spicy drumettes.

Finely crushed nacho chips	1/2 cup	125 mL
Finely chopped almonds	1/4 cup	60 mL
Chicken drumettes (or split chicken wings, tips discarded)	2 lbs.	900 g
Cooking spray		

PEACHY LIME SALSA

Peach jam	1/2 cup	125 mL
Salsa	1/2 cup	125 mL
Chopped fresh basil	2 tbsp.	30 mL
Lime juice	2 tbsp.	30 mL
Orange juice	2 tbsp.	30 mL

Combine chips and almonds in large resealable freezer bag. Add drumettes. Toss until coated. Arrange drumettes in single layer on greased wire rack set in foil-lined baking sheet with sides. Discard any remaining chip mixture.

Spray drumettes with cooking spray. Bake in 400°F (205°C) oven for about 45 minutes until fully cooked and internal temperature reaches 170°F (77°C).

Peachy Lime Salsa: Combine all 5 ingredients in small bowl. Makes about 1 1/3 cups (325 mL) salsa. Serve with drumettes. Makes about 16 drumettes (or 24 wing pieces).

1 drumette with 1 tbsp. (15 mL) salsa: 187 Calories; 11.1 g Total Fat (1.3 g Mono, 0.4 g Poly, 2.6 g Sat); 43 mg Cholesterol; 10 g Carbohydrate; trace Fibre; 11 g Protein; 99 mg Sodium

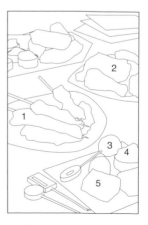

1. Lemon Grass Chicken Skewers, page 20
2. Salt And Pepper Wings, page 21
3. Corn Chicks, page 23
4. Chicken Salad Shells, page 13
5. Onion Apple Phyllo Rolls, page 15

Props courtesy of: Out of the Fire Studio
Pier 1 Imports
Stokes

Appetizers

Chicken Quesadillas

A 'dilla with a difference! Artichokes and cream cheese make a fantastically delicious statement in this great appetizer. Can also be served as a light lunch.

Garlic and herb cream cheese	1/4 cup	60 mL
Flour tortillas (9 inch, 22 cm, diameter)	4	4
Finely chopped cooked chicken (see Tip, page 26)	1 cup	250 mL
Lime juice	2 tbsp.	30 mL
Salt	1/8 tsp.	0.5 mL
Finely diced, seeded tomato	1/2 cup	125 mL
Thinly sliced green onion	1/4 cup	60 mL
Jar of marinated artichoke hearts, drained and chopped	6 oz.	170 mL
Grated jalapeño Monterey Jack cheese	1 cup	250 mL

Spread cream cheese evenly on each tortilla, almost to edge.

Place chicken in small bowl. Drizzle with lime juice. Sprinkle with salt. Stir. Spread chicken mixture over half of each tortilla.

Layer next 4 ingredients, in order given, over chicken mixture. Fold tortillas in half to cover filling. Press down lightly. Place on greased baking sheet. Bake in 425°F (220°C) oven for 10 to 12 minutes until cheese is melted and edges start to brown. Cut each quesadilla into 4 wedges. Makes 16 wedges.

1 wedge: 114 Calories; 5.0 g Total Fat (1.6 g Mono, 0.5 g Poly, 2.4 g Sat); 17 mg Cholesterol; 11 g Carbohydrate; 1 g Fibre; 6 g Protein; 206 mg Sodium

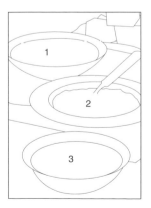

1. Black Bean Chicken Soup, page 32
2. Chicken Corn Chowder, page 34
3. Garden Noodle Soup, page 39

Props courtesy of: Cherison Enterprises Inc.
Casa Bugatti

Lemon Grass Chicken Skewers

Summertime get togethers are simply splashing with these splendid skewers—
and the light and refreshing salsa that accompanies them is superb!
A longer marinating time will intensify the flavour, so overnight is best.

Can of coconut milk	14 oz.	398 mL
Finely chopped lemon grass, bulb only (root and stalk removed),	2 1/2 tbsp.	37 mL
Brown sugar, packed	2 tbsp.	30 mL
Soy sauce	1 tbsp.	15 mL
Finely grated gingerroot	2 tsp.	10 mL
Garlic clove, minced (or 1/4 tsp., 1 mL, powder)	1	1
Boneless, skinless chicken thighs, cut in half lengthwise (about 1 lb., 454 g)	6	6
Bamboo skewers (8 inches, 20 cm, each), soaked in water for 10 minutes	12	12
CUCUMBER SALSA		
Lime juice	1/4 cup	60 mL
Cooking oil	2 tbsp.	30 mL
Granulated sugar	2 tbsp.	30 mL
Sweet chili sauce	2 tsp.	10 mL
Salt	1/4 tsp.	1 mL
Finely diced peeled cucumber, seeds removed	2 cups	500 mL
Finely chopped green onion	1/4 cup	60 mL
Chopped fresh cilantro or parsley	2 tbsp.	30 mL
Chopped salted peanuts	2 tbsp.	30 mL

Combine first 6 ingredients in small bowl.

Put chicken into large resealable freezer bag. Add coconut milk mixture. Seal bag. Turn until coated. Let stand in refrigerator for at least 4 hours or overnight, turning occasionally. Remove chicken. Transfer coconut milk mixture to small saucepan. Bring to a boil. Reduce heat to medium. Boil gently for at least 5 minutes, stirring occasionally.

(continued on next page)

Appetizers

Thread chicken, accordion-style, onto skewers. Preheat gas barbecue to medium (see Tip below). Cook chicken on greased grill for about 10 minutes, turning occasionally and brushing with coconut milk mixture, until no longer pink inside. Discard any remaining coconut milk mixture.

Cucumber Salsa: Combine first 5 ingredients in small bowl.

Add remaining 4 ingredients. Stir. Makes about 2 cups (500 mL) salsa. Serve salsa with skewers using slotted spoon. Makes 12 skewers.

1 skewer with 2 1/2 tbsp. (37 mL) salsa: 135 Calories; 9.5 g Total Fat (3.0 g Mono, 1.6 g Poly, 4.2 g Sat); 25 mg Cholesterol; 6 g Carbohydrate; trace Fibre; 8 g Protein; 156 mg Sodium

Pictured on page 17.

Salt And Pepper Wings

Forget wing night at the local pub. No pub can top these simple and tasty tidbits. Say "Cheers," and dig right in! No tip required.

Split chicken wings, tips discarded (or chicken drumettes)	2 lbs.	900 g
Soy sauce	2 tbsp.	30 mL
Montreal steak spice	2 tsp.	10 mL
Coarsely ground pepper	1/2 tsp.	2 mL
Lemon pepper	1/2 tsp.	2 mL

Arrange wing pieces in single layer on greased wire rack set in foil-lined baking sheet with sides.

Brush soy sauce on both sides of wing pieces. Sprinkle remaining 3 ingredients on both sides of wing pieces. Bake in 425°F (220°C) oven for about 40 minutes, turning at halftime, until crisp golden brown and fully cooked. Makes about 24 wing pieces (or 16 drumettes).

1 wing: 86 Calories; 6.0 g Total Fat (0 g Mono, 0 g Poly, 1.6 g Sat); 28 mg Cholesterol; trace Carbohydrate; trace Fibre; 7 g Protein; 190 mg Sodium

Pictured on page 17.

 Too cold to barbecue? Use the broiler instead! Your food should cook in about the same length of time and remember to turn or baste as directed. Set your oven rack so that the food is about 3 to 4 inches (7.5 to 10 cm) away from the element. For most ovens, this is the top rack.

Stuffed Grape Leaves

In Greece, they're commonly called dolmades but you can just call them delicious. Everyone will agree that these chicken and rice-stuffed grape leaves are simply de-vine! Serve with lemon wedges and our delicious Cucumber Dill Dip that also goes great with cut-up veggies.

Long grain white rice	1/2 cup	125 mL
Boiling water	1 cup	250 mL
Chopped pine nuts, toasted (see Tip, page 13), optional	3 tbsp.	50 mL
Parsley flakes	2 tsp.	10 mL
Dried oregano	1 tsp.	5 mL
Garlic powder	1/2 tsp.	2 mL
Dried rosemary, crushed	1/4 tsp.	1 mL
Salt	1/4 tsp.	1 mL
Pepper	1/8 tsp	0.5 mL
Lean ground chicken	1/2 lb.	225 g
Grape leaves, rinsed and drained, tough stems removed (see Note)	24	24
Prepared chicken broth	1 cup	250 mL
CUCUMBER DILL DIP		
Sour cream	1 cup	250 mL
Grated English cucumber (with peel), squeezed dry	1/2 cup	125 mL
White vinegar	1 tsp.	5 mL
Garlic clove, minced (or 1/4 tsp., 1 mL, powder)	1	1
Chopped fresh dill	1 tsp.	5 mL
Salt	1/4 tsp.	1 mL
Pepper	1/8 tsp.	0.5 mL

Put rice into small bowl. Add water. Stir. Let stand for 15 minutes. Drain. Rinse with cold water. Drain well.

Combine next 7 ingredients in medium bowl.

Add chicken and rice. Mix well.

(continued on next page)

Appetizers

Place 1 leaf on work surface, vein-side up, stem-side (bottom of leaf) closest to you. Place about 1 tbsp. (15 mL) of chicken mixture about 1/2 inch (12 mm) from bottom of leaf. Fold bottom of leaf over chicken mixture. Fold in sides. Roll up from bottom to enclose filling. Place seam-side down in large saucepan. Repeat with remaining leaves and filling.

Pour broth over stuffed leaves. Bring to a boil. Reduce heat to medium-low. Simmer, covered, for 35 minutes. Remove from heat. Let stand, covered, for 15 to 20 minutes until internal temperature reaches 175°F (80°C) and liquid is almost all absorbed.

Cucumber Dill Dip: Combine all 7 ingredients in small bowl. Makes about 1 cup (250 mL) dip. Serve with stuffed leaves. Makes 24 stuffed leaves.

1 stuffed leaf with 2 tsp. (10 mL) dip: 65 Calories; 3.8 g Total Fat (0.3 g Mono, 0.3 g Poly, 1.3 g Sat); 7 mg Cholesterol; 4 g Carbohydrate; trace Fibre; 3 g Protein; 205 mg Sodium

Note: Grape leaves can generally be found in the import section of your grocery store.

Corn Chicks

Ordinary chicken meatballs are transformed into golden nuggets with a crispy coating of corn chips. Serve with your favourite dipping sauce.

Large egg, fork-beaten	1	1
Fine dry bread crumbs	1/2 cup	125 mL
Seasoned salt	1/2 tsp.	2 mL
Poultry seasoning	1/4 tsp.	1 mL
Pepper	1/8 tsp.	0.5 mL
Lean ground chicken	1 lb.	454 g
Finely crushed corn chips	1 cup	250 mL

Combine first 5 ingredients in large bowl.

Add chicken. Mix well. Roll into 1 inch (2.5 cm) balls.

Put chips into small shallow dish. Roll each meatball in corn chips until coated. Discard any remaining chips. Arrange meatballs on greased baking sheet with sides. Bake in 350°F (175°C) oven for about 25 minutes until fully cooked and internal temperature reaches 175°F (80°C). Makes about 28 meatballs.

1 meatball: 57 Calories; 3.0 g Total Fat (0.1 g Mono, trace Poly, 0.1 g Sat); 6.7 mg Cholesterol; 3 g Carbohydrate; trace Fibre; 3 g Protein; 84 mg Sodium

Pictured on page 17.

Potstickers

Do you fancy chicken and dumplings? How about chicken in dumplings?
As fun to make as they are to eat.

DIPPING SAUCE

Water	1/2 cup	125 mL
Rice vinegar	2 tbsp.	30 mL
Soy sauce	2 tbsp.	30 mL
Sweet chili sauce	2 tbsp.	30 mL
Sesame oil	1 tbsp.	15 mL

POTSTICKERS

Dried shiitake mushrooms	6	6
Boiling water	1 cup	250 mL
Lean ground chicken	1/2 lb.	225 g
Finely chopped green onion	1/3 cup	75 mL
Soy sauce	2 tbsp.	30 mL
Finely chopped fresh cilantro or parsley (or 1 1/2 tsp., 7 mL, dried)	2 tbsp.	30 mL
Finely grated gingerroot (or 3/4 tsp., 4 mL, ground ginger)	1 tbsp.	15 mL
Garlic cloves, minced (or 1/2 tsp., 2 mL, powder)	2	2
Sesame oil	1 tsp.	5 mL
Dried crushed chilies	1/4 tsp.	1 mL
Water	1/4 cup	60 mL
Cornstarch	1 tbsp.	15 mL
Round dumpling wrappers	24	24
Cooking oil	3 tbsp.	50 mL
Water	3 tbsp.	50 mL

Dipping Sauce: Combine all 5 ingredients in small bowl. Stir. Makes about 1 cup (250 mL) sauce.

Potstickers: Put mushrooms into small heatproof bowl. Add boiling water. Stir. Let stand for about 20 minutes until softened. Drain. Remove and discard stems. Finely chop caps. Set aside.

Combine next 8 ingredients in medium bowl.

(continued on next page)

Stir first amount of water into cornstarch in small cup. Place 1 wrapper on work surface. Cover remaining wrappers with damp towel to prevent drying. Place about 1 tbsp. (15 mL) chicken mixture in centre of wrapper. Dampen edges of wrapper with cornstarch mixture. Fold in half over filling. Crimp edges to seal. Cover filled dumplings with separate damp towel to prevent drying. Repeat with remaining wrappers, chicken mixture and cornstarch mixture.

Heat cooking oil in large frying pan on medium until very hot. Arrange dumplings in single layer in pan. Cook for 3 to 5 minutes until bottoms of dumplings are golden. Turn. Add second amount of water. Cook, covered, for about 5 minutes until internal temperature reaches 175°F (80°C), water is evaporated and bottoms of dumplings are crisp. Transfer to plate. Serve immediately with dipping sauce. Makes 24 potstickers.

1 potsticker with 2 tsp. (10 mL) sauce: 72 Calories; 3.9 g Total Fat (1.3 g Mono, 0.9 g Poly, 0.3 g Sat); 1 mg Cholesterol; 6 g Carbohydrate; trace Fibre; 3 g Protein; 291 mg Sodium

Pesto Chicken Tarts

Which came first, the chicken or the egg? In this recipe they come together. Pesto and cheese make this tasty mini quiche hard to beat.

Large eggs	4	4
Milk	1/2 cup	125 mL
Basil pesto	1/4 cup	60 mL
Grated Parmesan cheese	1/4 cup	60 mL
Pepper	1/4 tsp.	1 mL
Finely chopped cooked chicken (see Tip, page 26)	1 cup	250 mL
Unbaked tart shells (unsweetened)	16	16
Grated Parmesan cheese	4 tsp.	20 mL

Beat first 5 ingredients in medium bowl until frothy.

Add chicken. Stir.

Place tart shells on ungreased baking sheet with sides. Spoon about 2 tbsp. (30 mL) of egg mixture into each tart shell. Sprinkle tarts with second amount of cheese. Bake in 375°F (190°C) oven for about 25 minutes until pastry is golden and wooden pick inserted in centre comes out clean. Makes 16 tarts.

1 tart: 206 Calories; 11.5 g Total Fat (3.5 g Mono, 0.3 g Poly, 2.8 g Sat); 56 mg Cholesterol; 18 g Carbohydrate; trace Fibre; 7 g Protein; 177 mg Sodium

Appetizers

Chicken Salad Amandine

Ants in your pants? Who cares? When you have the perfect picnic salad, nothing can ruin your outing. Doubles easily for larger crowds. If you're making the salad in advance, wait until just before serving to add the dressing.

Water	4 cups	1 L
Salt	1/2 tsp.	2 mL
Elbow macaroni	1 cup	250 mL
Chopped cooked chicken (see Tip)	2 cups	500 mL
Diced medium Cheddar cheese	1/2 cup	125 mL
Sliced celery	1/2 cup	125 mL
Sliced natural almonds, toasted (see Tip, page 13)	1/2 cup	125 mL
Jar of sliced pimento, well drained and chopped	2 oz.	57 mL
Sliced green onion	3 tbsp.	50 mL
Salt	1/4 tsp.	1 mL
Pepper	1/8 tsp.	0.5 mL
DRESSING:		
Salad dressing (or mayonnaise)	1/2 cup	125 mL
Sweet pickle relish	1 tbsp.	15 mL
White vinegar	1 tbsp.	15 mL
Granulated sugar	1 1/2 tsp.	7 mL

Combine water and salt in large saucepan. Bring to a boil. Add macaroni. Boil, uncovered, for 6 to 8 minutes, stirring occasionally, until tender but firm. Drain. Rinse with cold water. Drain. Transfer to large bowl.

Add next 8 ingredients. Toss.

Dressing: Combine all 4 ingredients in small bowl. Makes about 3/4 cup (175 mL) dressing. Pour over chicken mixture. Toss. Makes about 6 cups (1.5 L).

1 cup (250 mL): 405 Calories; 25.4 g Total Fat (12.9 g Mono, 6.9 g Poly, 4.6 g Sat); 56 mg Cholesterol; 26 g Carbohydrate; 2 g Fibre; 18 g Protein; 507 mg Sodium

tip   Don't have any leftover chicken? Start with 2 boneless, skinless chicken breast halves (4 – 6 oz., 113 – 117 g, each). Place in large frying pan with 1 cup (250 mL) water or chicken broth. Simmer, covered, for 12 to 14 minutes until no longer pink inside. Drain. Chop. Makes about 2 cups (500 mL) of cooked chicken.

Salads & Soups

Peach And Chicken Salad

They'll all think you're just peachy-keen when you make the scene with this delightfully sweet and refreshing summer salad.

Boneless, skinless chicken breast halves	1 lb.	454 g
Seasoned salt	1 tsp.	5 mL
Pepper	1/2 tsp.	2 mL
Cut or torn romaine lettuce, lightly packed	6 cups	1.5 L
Chopped red pepper	2 cups	500 mL
Can of sliced peaches, drained and chopped	14 oz.	398 mL
Pecan pieces, toasted (see Tip, page 13)	1/2 cup	125 mL
Thinly sliced green onion	1/2 cup	125 mL
Chopped fresh parsley	1/4 cup	60 mL
PEACH VINAIGRETTE		
White vinegar	3 tbsp.	50 mL
Peach jam	2 tbsp.	30 mL
Cooking oil	1 tbsp.	15 mL
Garlic clove, minced (or 1/4 tsp., 1 mL, powder)	1	1
Red wine vinegar	1 tsp.	5 mL
Salt	1/4 tsp.	1 mL
Pepper	1/8 tsp.	0.5 mL

Sprinkle chicken with seasoned salt and pepper. Preheat gas barbecue to medium-high (see Tip, page 21). Cook chicken on greased grill for about 6 to 8 minutes per side until fully cooked and internal temperature reaches 170°F (77°C). Remove to cutting board. Let stand for 5 minutes. Cut crosswise into 1/2 inch (12 mm) strips. Cool slightly.

Put next 6 ingredients into extra-large bowl. Toss gently. Add chicken.

Peach Vinaigrette: Combine all 7 ingredients in jar with tight-fitting lid. Shake well. Makes about 1/3 cup (75 mL) dressing. Drizzle over salad. Toss gently. Makes about 10 cups (2.5 L).

1 cup (250 mL): 156 Calories; 6.5 g Total Fat (3.4 g Mono, 1.9 g Poly, 0.7 g Sat); 26 mg Cholesterol; 14 g Carbohydrate; 3 g Fibre; 12 g Protein; 231 mg Sodium

Pictured on page 35.

Vermicelli Chicken Salads

Want to get fresh? There's nothing fresher than this cool treat. Doubles easily.

TERIYAKI LIME DRESSING

Lime juice	1/2 cup	125 mL
Sweet chili sauce	1/2 cup	125 mL
Thick teriyaki basting sauce	1/2 cup	125 mL

SALAD

Boneless, skinless chicken breast halves	1 lb.	454 g
Prepared chicken broth	4 cups	1 L
Thick teriyaki basting sauce	2 tbsp.	30 mL
Finely grated gingerroot	2 tsp.	10 mL
Boiling water	6 cups	1.5 L
Rice vermicelli	8 1/2 oz.	250 g
Shredded suey choy (Chinese cabbage)	4 cups	1 L
Sliced English cucumber (with peel)	1 1/2 cups	375 mL
Grated carrot	1 cup	250 mL
Chopped fresh mint	1/3 cup	75 mL
Fresh bean sprouts	2 cups	500 mL
Chopped green onion	1/4 cup	60 mL
Chopped salted peanuts	1/4 cup	60 mL

Teriyaki Lime Dressing: Combine all 3 ingredients in small bowl. Makes about 1 1/2 cups (375 mL) dressing.

Salad: Combine first 4 ingredients in large saucepan. Bring to a boil. Reduce heat to medium-low. Simmer, uncovered, for about 15 minutes until chicken is fully cooked and internal temperature reaches 170°F (77°C). Remove from heat. Transfer chicken with slotted spoon to small bowl. Cool. Reserve broth mixture.

Add boiling water and vermicelli to reserved broth mixture. Let stand for 5 to 10 minutes until vermicelli is softened. Drain. Rinse with cold water. Drain well. Return to same saucepan. Add 1 cup (250 mL) Teriyaki Lime Dressing. Toss.

Arrange next 4 ingredients on 4 individual serving plates. Spoon noodles over top. Cut chicken crosswise into 1/8 inch (3 mm) strips. Arrange over noodles.

(continued on next page)

Sprinkle remaining 3 ingredients over chicken. Drizzle remaining dressing over salads. Makes 4 salads—enough to feed you and 3 happy friends.

1 salad: 602 Calories; 8.3 g Total Fat (3.3 g Mono, 2.3 g Poly, 1.6 g Sat); 66 mg Cholesterol; 83 g Carbohydrate; 8 g Fibre; 43 g Protein; 2414 mg Sodium

Pictured on page 35.

Cherry Chicken Salad

Rich and colourful, this cheery cherry salad makes a delicious lunch or an attractive supper side. Feel free to be creative and use other dried fruit such as cranberries, chopped figs or apricots.

Mixed salad greens, lightly packed	8 cups	2 L
Dried cherries	1 cup	250 mL
Sliced natural almonds, toasted (see Tip, page 13)	3/4 cup	175 mL
Cooking oil	1 tsp.	5 mL
Boneless, skinless chicken breast halves, cut crosswise into 1/2 inch (12 mm) slices	1/2 lb.	225 g
Salt, sprinkle		
Pepper, sprinkle		
PESTO DRESSING		
Red wine vinegar	1/4 cup	60 mL
Basil pesto	3 tbsp.	50 mL
Olive (or cooking) oil	1 tbsp.	15 mL

Put first 3 ingredients into large bowl. Toss.

Heat cooking oil in small frying pan on medium-high. Add chicken. Sprinkle with salt and pepper. Cook for about 5 minutes, stirring occasionally, until chicken is no longer pink inside. Remove from heat. Cool. Add to salad mixture. Toss.

Pesto Dressing: Whisk all 3 ingredients in small bowl until combined. Makes about 1/3 cup (75 mL) dressing. Drizzle over salad. Toss. Makes about 8 cups (2 L).

1 cup (250 mL): 204 Calories; 10.3 g Total Fat (4.5 g Mono, 1.6 g Poly, 1.2 g Sat); 18 mg Cholesterol; 16 g Carbohydrate; 4 g Fibre; 11 g Protein; 82 mg Sodium

Hawaiian Chicken Salads

The fresh, fruity flavours of the islands will have you hanging 10 in no time.

Thick teriyaki basting sauce	1/3 cup	75 mL
Boneless, skinless chicken breast halves (4 – 6 oz., 113 – 170 g, each)	4	4
Spring mix lettuce, lightly packed	8 cups	2 L
Frozen mango pieces, thawed, drained and chopped	1 1/2 cups	375 mL
Frozen pineapple pieces, thawed and drained	1 1/2 cups	375 mL
Chopped raw macadamia nuts, toasted (see Tip, page 13)	1/2 cup	125 mL
Shredded coconut, toasted (see Tip, page 13)	2 tbsp.	30 mL
Raspberry vinaigrette	1/2 cup	125 mL

Brush teriyaki sauce on both sides of chicken. Preheat gas barbecue to medium-high (see Tip, page 21). Cook chicken on greased grill for 6 to 8 minutes per side, basting with remaining teriyaki sauce, until chicken is fully cooked and internal temperature reaches 170°F (77°C). Remove to cutting board. Cut chicken diagonally into 1/2 inch (12 mm) strips. Cool slightly.

Arrange lettuce on 4 individual serving plates. Arrange one sliced breast over lettuce on each plate. Arrange mango and pineapple over chicken.

Sprinkle macadamia nuts and coconut over top. Drizzle vinaigrette over salads. Makes 4 salads.

1 salad: 461 Calories; 16.6 g Total Fat (10.5 g Mono, 0.9 g Poly, 3.9 g Sat); 66 mg Cholesterol; 51 g Carbohydrate; 6 g Fibre; 30 g Protein; 929 mg Sodium

Pictured on page 35.

Paré Pointer
Is an octopus really an eight-sided cat?

Salads & Soups

Creamy Curry Chicken Salad

*Never bland, never boring—you'll find that a little spice
is extra nice in a chicken salad. Serve with warm garlic bread.*

Boneless, skinless chicken breast halves, cut crosswise into thin strips (see Tip)	1/2 lb.	225 g
Italian dressing	1/3 cup	75 mL
Olive (or cooking) oil	1 tsp.	5 mL
Cut or torn romaine lettuce, lightly packed	3 cups	750 mL
Cherry (or grape) tomatoes, halved	2 cups	500 mL
Can of artichoke hearts, drained and halved	14 oz.	398 mL
Kalamata (or black) olives, halved	16	16
CREAMY CURRY DRESSING		
Mayonnaise	1/3 cup	75 mL
Finely chopped fresh basil	2 tbsp.	30 mL
Lemon juice	2 tbsp.	30 mL
Liquid honey	1 tbsp.	15 mL
Chili paste (sambal oelek)	1 tsp.	5 mL
Curry powder	1 tsp.	5 mL

Stir chicken and Italian dressing in medium bowl until coated.
Let stand, covered, in refrigerator for 1 hour, stirring occasionally.
Drain and discard dressing.

Heat olive oil in small frying pan on medium-high. Add chicken. Cook for
about 5 minutes, stirring occasionally, until no longer pink inside. Transfer
to large bowl. Chill. Add next 4 ingredients. Toss.

Creamy Curry Dressing: Combine all 6 ingredients in small bowl.
Makes about 1/2 cup (125 mL) of dressing. Drizzle over salad. Toss. Makes
about 8 cups (2 L).

*1 cup (250 mL: 196 Calories; 13.5 g Total Fat (7.8 g Mono, 3.9 g Poly, 1.4 g Sat);
25 mg Cholesterol; 11 g Carbohydrate; 4 g Fibre; 9 g Protein; 308 mg Sodium*

 tip To slice meat easily, place in freezer for about 30 minutes until
just starting to freeze. If using from frozen state, partially thaw
before cutting.

Black Bean Chicken Soup

This salsa-spiced bean soup will get you shaking your maracas in no time!
Garnish with a dollop of sour cream and serve with a slice of cornbread.

Cooking oil	1 tbsp.	15 mL
Chopped onion	2 cups	500 mL
Boneless, skinless chicken thighs, chopped	1/2 lb.	225 g
Chopped fresh jalapeño pepper (see Tip, page 33)	2 tbsp.	30 mL
Garlic cloves, minced (or 3/4 tsp., 4 mL, powder)	3	3
Dried oregano	1 tsp.	5 mL
Ground coriander	1/2 tsp.	2 mL
Ground cumin	1/2 tsp.	2 mL
Prepared chicken broth	4 cups	1 L
Bay leaves	2	2
Can of diced tomatoes (with juice)	28 oz.	796 mL
Can of black beans, rinsed and drained	19 oz.	540 mL
Barbecue sauce	1/3 cup	75 mL
Salsa	1/4 cup	60 mL
Chopped fresh cilantro or parsley	1/4 cup	60 mL
Lime juice	3 tbsp.	50 mL
Pepper	1/4 tsp.	1 mL

Heat cooking oil in Dutch oven or large pot on medium. Add next 7 ingredients. Cook, uncovered, for about 10 minutes, stirring occasionally, until onion is softened and chicken is no longer pink.

Add broth and bay leaves. Stir. Bring to a boil. Reduce heat to medium-low. Simmer, covered, for 10 minutes to blend flavours.

Process next 4 ingredients in blender or food processor until almost smooth. Add to soup. Stir. Bring to a boil. Reduce heat to medium-low. Simmer for 5 minutes to blend flavors. Discard bay leaves.

Add remaining 3 ingredients. Stir. Makes about 10 1/2 cups (2.6 L).

1 cup (250 mL): 162 Calories; 3.9 g Total Fat (1.7 g Mono, 1.0 g Poly, 0.8 g Sat); 14 mg Cholesterol; 21 g Carbohydrate; 4 g Fibre; 12 g Protein; 723 mg Sodium

Pictured on page 18.

Pictured on page 18.

Shredded Chicken Soup

Turn notions of classic chicken soup upside down
with this shredded version studded with pimientoes.

Water	10 cups	2.5 L
Chicken legs, back attached, skin removed	2 lbs.	900 g
Bone-in chicken breast halves, skin removed	1 lb.	454 g
Chopped carrot	1 cup	250 mL
Chopped celery	1 cup	250 mL
Chopped onion	1 cup	250 mL
Chicken bouillon powder	2 tbsp.	30 mL
Bay leaf	1	1
Dried thyme	1/2 tsp.	2 mL
Salt	1/4 tsp.	1 mL
Pepper	1/4 tsp.	1 mL
Cayenne pepper	1/8 tsp.	0.5 mL
Jar of sliced pimiento, well drained	2 oz.	57 mL
Water	1/2 cup	125 mL
All-purpose flour	2 tbsp.	30 mL

Combine first 12 ingredients in Dutch oven or large pot. Bring to a boil. Reduce heat to medium-low. Simmer, uncovered, for about 1 1/2 hours, stirring occasionally, until chicken is tender and starts to fall off bones. Remove from heat. Transfer chicken and bones to cutting board using slotted spoon. Remove chicken from bones. Discard bones. Chop chicken. Set aside. Discard bay leaf. Skim and discard fat from broth.

Add pimiento. Carefully process with hand blender or in blender until smooth. Add chicken. Bring to a boil. Reduce heat to medium.

Stir second amount of water into flour in small bowl until smooth. Add to soup. Stir. Cook for about 5 minutes, stirring occasionally, until thickened. Makes about 10 cups (2.5 L).

1 cup (250 mL): 179 Calories; 5.2 g Total Fat (1.6 g Mono, 1.3 g Poly, 1.3 g Sat); 94 mg Cholesterol; 5 g Carbohydrate; 1 g Fibre; 26 g Protein; 728 mg Sodium

 Hot peppers contain capsaicin in the seeds and ribs. Removing the seeds and ribs will reduce the heat. Wear rubber gloves when handling hot peppers and avoid touching your eyes. Wash your hands well afterwards.

Chicken Corn Chowder

Consider this to be the food version of a warm, comforting hug.

Cooking oil	1 tbsp.	15 mL
Boneless, skinless chicken breast halves, chopped	1 lb.	454 g
Chopped onion	1 cup	250 mL
Chopped deli ham	3/4 cup	175 mL
Chopped celery	1/2 cup	125 mL
Dried crushed chilies	1/2 tsp.	2 mL
Prepared chicken broth	4 cups	1 L
Frozen kernel corn	2 1/2 cups	625 mL
Chopped peeled potato	2 cups	500 mL
Diced red pepper	1 cup	250 mL
Sliced green onion	1/2 cup	125 mL
Sprigs of fresh thyme	2	2
Bay leaf	1	1
Salt	1/4 tsp.	1 mL
Can of evaporated milk	13 1/2 oz.	385 mL
All-purpose flour	3 tbsp.	50 mL

Heat cooking oil in Dutch oven or large pot on medium. Add next 5 ingredients. Stir. Cook, uncovered, for about 10 minutes, stirring occasionally, until chicken is no longer pink and vegetables are softened.

Add next 8 ingredients. Stir. Bring to a boil. Reduce heat to medium-low. Simmer, covered, for about 15 minutes until potato is tender.

Whisk evaporated milk and flour in small bowl until smooth. Stir into soup. Increase heat to medium. Heat and stir for about 5 minutes until boiling and thickened. Discard thyme sprigs and bay leaf. Makes about 10 cups (2.5 L).

1 cup (250 mL): 225 Calories; 6.2 g Total Fat (2.2 g Mono, 1.0 g Poly, "2.3 g Sat); 42 mg Cholesterol; 25 g Carbohydrate; 2 g Fibre; 9 g Protein; 580 mg Sodium

Pictured on page 18.

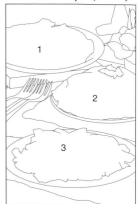

1. Hawaiian Chicken Salads, page 30
2. Vermicelli Chicken Salads, page 28
3. Peach And Chicken Salad, page 27

Props courtesy of: Dansk Gifts
Totally Bamboo
Winners Stores

Chicken Pumpkin Soup

Pumpkins abound in October—put them to good use in this elegant soup.

Butter (or hard margarine)	2 tbsp.	30 mL
Boneless, skinless chicken breast halves, cut in 1/2 inch (12 mm) cubes	6 oz.	170 g
Finely chopped onion	2 1/2 cups	625 mL
Garlic cloves, minced	3	3
Bay leaves	2	2
Salt	1/4 tsp.	1 mL
Pepper	1/4 tsp.	1 mL
Prepared chicken broth	3 cups	750 mL
Can of pure pumpkin (no spices)	14 oz.	398 mL
Chopped fresh dill (or 1 1/2 tsp., 7 mL, dried)	2 tbsp.	30 mL
Sour cream	1/2 cup	125 mL
Chopped salted, roasted shelled pumpkin seeds	1/4 cup	60 mL
Chopped fresh dill (or 1/4 tsp., 1 mL, dried)	1 tsp.	5 mL

Melt butter in large saucepan on medium. Add next 6 ingredients. Cook, uncovered, for about 10 minutes, stirring occasionally, until onion is very soft and chicken is no longer pink.

Add next 3 ingredients. Stir. Bring to a boil. Reduce heat to medium-low. Simmer, covered, for 5 minutes to blend flavours. Discard bay leaves. Remove from heat.

Stir sour cream into soup. Makes about 7 cups (1.75 L) soup.

Sprinkle pumpkin seeds and dill over individual servings. Serves 4.

1 serving: 341 Calories; 18.8 g Total Fat (4.0 g Mono, 3.4 g Poly, 8.9 g Sat); 60 mg Cholesterol; 23 g Carbohydrate; 5 g Fibre; 21 g Protein; 892 mg Sodium

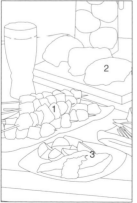

1. Pineapple Rum Kabobs, page 41
2. Cedar Plank Chicken, page 48
3. Chicken Aztec, page 49

Props courtesy of: Pfaltzgraff Canada
Stokes

Chicken Gumbo

This southern favourite is sure to pique the hot-sauce lover's interest.

Cooking oil	1 tbsp.	15 mL
Boneless, skinless chicken breast halves, cut into 1 inch (2.5 cm) cubes	1/2 lb.	225 g
Cooking oil	3 tbsp.	50 mL
All-purpose flour	3 tbsp.	50 mL
Can of stewed tomatoes	14 oz.	398 mL
Tomato paste (see Tip, page 105)	2 tbsp.	30 mL
Paprika	1 tsp.	5 mL
Prepared chicken broth	4 cups	1 L
Fresh (or frozen, thawed) okra, cut into 1/2 inch (12 mm) slices	2 cups	500 mL
Diced celery	1 cup	250 mL
Diced green pepper	1 cup	250 mL
Diced onion	1 cup	250 mL
Sliced smoked ham sausage	1 cup	250 mL
Garlic cloves, minced (or 1/2 tsp., 2 mL, powder)	2	2
Bay leaf	1	1
Louisiana hot sauce	1 – 2 tsp.	5 – 10 mL
Dried thyme	1 tsp.	5 mL
Long grain white rice	1/2 cup	125 mL
Frozen, uncooked medium shrimp (peeled and deveined), thawed (optional)	1/2 lb.	225 g

Heat first amount of cooking oil in Dutch oven or large pot on medium-high. Add chicken. Cook, uncovered, for about 3 minutes, stirring occasionally, until lightly browned. Transfer to small bowl. Set aside.

Heat second amount of cooking oil in same pot on medium. Add flour. Heat and stir for about 3 minutes until deep golden brown.

Slowly add next 3 ingredients, stirring constantly and breaking up tomatoes with spoon, until combined. Heat and stir for 1 minute.

Add next 11 ingredients and chicken. Stir. Bring to a boil. Reduce heat to medium-low. Simmer, covered, for 45 to 60 minutes, stirring occasionally, until rice and chicken are tender. Discard bay leaf.

(continued on next page)

Salads & Soups

Add shrimp. Stir. Cook, covered, for about 3 minutes until shrimp turn pink.
Makes about 10 cups (2.5 L).

1 cup (250 mL): 220 Calories; 11.3 g Total Fat (5.8 g Mono, 2.4 g Poly, 2.4 g Sat);
23 mg Cholesterol; 17 g Carbohydrate; 2 g Fibre; 13 g Protein; 667 mg Sodium

Garden Noodle Soup

All the long hours spent toiling in your garden finally pay off! Fantastically fresh!

Cooking oil	2 tsp.	10 mL
Boneless, skinless chicken breast halves, chopped	1 lb.	454 g
Chopped zucchini (with peel)	1 cup	250 mL
Chopped onion	1/2 cup	125 mL
Chopped carrot	1/3 cup	75 mL
Prepared chicken broth	4 cups	1 L
Chopped tomato	1 1/2 cups	375 mL
Medium egg noodles	3/4 cup	175 mL
Chopped fresh asparagus	1/2 cup	125 mL
Sprig of fresh thyme (or 1/8 tsp., 0.5 mL dried)	1	1
Salt	1/4 tsp.	1 mL
Pepper	1/8 tsp.	0.5 mL
Chopped fresh spinach leaves, lightly packed	1 cup	250 mL
Chopped fresh basil	1 tbsp.	15 mL

Heat cooking oil in large saucepan or Dutch oven on medium-high.
Add chicken. Stir. Cook, uncovered, for about 5 minutes, stirring
occasionally, until no longer pink.

Add next 3 ingredients. Reduce heat to medium. Cook for about
5 minutes, stirring often, until onion is softened.

Add next 7 ingredients. Stir. Bring to a boil. Reduce heat to medium-low.
Simmer, partially covered, for about 8 minutes until noodles are tender
but firm. Discard thyme sprig.

Add spinach and basil. Heat and stir for 2 to 3 minutes until spinach
is wilted. Makes about 7 cups (1.75 L).

1 cup (250 mL): 143 Calories; 3.5 g Total Fat (1.4 g Mono, 0.9 g Poly, 0.7 g Sat); 41 mg Cholesterol;
8 g Carbohydrate; 2 g Fibre; 19 g Protein; 578 mg Sodium

Pictured on page 18.

Caribbean Chicken

Life is easy when ja-makin' some of this Caribbean-influenced grilled chicken.
Similar to Jamaican jerk chicken but much milder. The heat is beautifully
tempered by a fresh, fruity topping filled with papaya and avocado.

Onion powder	1 1/2 tsp.	7 mL
Dried thyme	1 tsp.	5 mL
Granulated sugar	1 tsp.	5 mL
Ground allspice	1/2 tsp.	2 mL
Salt	1/2 tsp.	2 mL
Pepper	1/2 tsp.	2 mL
Cayenne pepper	1/4 tsp.	1 mL
Ground cinnamon	1/4 tsp.	1 mL
Ground nutmeg	1/4 tsp.	1 mL
Diced avocado	2 cups	500 mL
Diced papaya	1 1/2 cups	375 mL
Lime juice	3 tbsp.	50 mL
Orange juice	3 tbsp.	50 mL
Grated orange zest	1 tsp.	5 mL
Salt	1/4 tsp.	1 mL
Orange juice	1 1/2 tbsp.	25 mL
Boneless, skinless chicken breast halves	4	4
(4 – 6 oz., 113 – 170 g, each)		

Combine first 9 ingredients in small bowl. Transfer 1 tsp. (5 mL) to medium bowl. Set aside remaining spice mixture.

Add next 6 ingredients to spice mixture in medium bowl. Toss to combine.

Add second amount of orange juice to remaining spice mixture in small bowl. Stir to form a paste. Rub on both sides of chicken. Let stand, covered, in refrigerator for 1 hour. Preheat gas barbecue to medium (see Tip, page 21). Cook chicken on greased grill for about 10 minutes per side until fully cooked and internal temperature reaches 170°F (77°C). Remove to cutting board. Cut chicken crosswise into 1/4 inch (6 mm) strips. Transfer to serving platter. Spoon papaya mixture over chicken. Serves 4.

1 serving: 289 Calories; 13.1 g Total Fat (7.8 g Mono, 1.8 g Poly, 2.2 g Sat); 66 mg Cholesterol; 17 g Carbohydrate; 6 g Fibre; 30 g Protein; 510 mg Sodium

Pineapple Rum Kabobs

There's a reason rum runners risked it all. For fabulously flavoured chicken,
of course! OK, maybe we're stretching it a little but when your guests
taste these rum-laced kabobs, we're sure they'll brave almost anything
for a second helping. Use a ripe pineapple for best results.

Dark (navy) rum	1/4 cup	60 mL
Lime juice	1/4 cup	60 mL
Liquid honey	1/4 cup	60 mL
Brown sugar, packed	1 tbsp.	15 mL
Dijon mustard	1 tbsp.	15 mL
Cooking oil	2 tsp.	10 mL
Boneless, skinless chicken breast halves, cut into 36, 1 inch (2.5 cm) pieces	1 1/2 lbs.	680 g
Medium pineapple, cut into 36, 1 inch (2.5 cm) pieces	1	1
Bamboo skewers (8 inches, 20 cm, each), soaked in water for 10 minutes	12	12

Whisk first 6 ingredients in small bowl. Pour into large resealable freezer bag.

Add chicken. Seal bag. Turn until coated. Let stand in refrigerator for
1 hour, turning occasionally. Remove chicken. Transfer rum mixture to
small saucepan. Bring to a boil on medium. Reduce heat to medium-low.
Simmer, uncovered, for at least 5 minutes.

Thread 3 pieces of chicken and 3 pieces of pineapple alternately onto each
skewer. Preheat gas barbecue to medium (see Tip, page 21). Cook kabobs
on greased grill for about 12 minutes, turning occasionally and brushing
with reserved rum mixture, until chicken is no longer pink inside. Makes
12 kabobs.

1 kabob: 128 Calories; 1.7 g Total Fat (0.7 g Mono, 0.5 g Poly, 0.3 g Sat); 33 mg Cholesterol;
12 g Carbohydrate; 1 g Fibre; 13 g Protein; 49 mg Sodium

Pictured on page 36.

Paré Pointer

If your basement gets water in it, change your shoes. Wear pumps.

Hickory Chicken and Apricots

Forgo the smokehouse—we tell you exactly how to get that genuine hickory taste using your barbecue. You won't believe how well apricots and pecans combine with a smoky hickory flavour.

APRICOT STUFFING

Can of apricot halves in light syrup, drained and syrup reserved, finely chopped (see Note 1)	14 oz.	398 mL
Fresh bread crumbs	2/3 cup	150 mL
Chopped pecans, toasted (see Tip, page 13)	1/2 cup	125 mL
Finely chopped onion	1/2 cup	125 mL
Chopped fresh parsley (or 2 1/4 tsp., 11 mL, flakes)	3 tbsp.	50 mL
Brown sugar, packed	2 tsp.	10 mL
Salt	1/4 tsp.	1 mL
Pepper, sprinkle		
Whole chicken	4 lbs.	1.8 kg
Hickory wood chips (see Note 2)	1 1/2 cup	375 mL
Water		
Reserved syrup from apricots	2/3 cup	150 mL
Soy sauce	1 1/2 tbsp.	25 mL
Dijon mustard	1 tbsp.	15 mL
Liquid honey	1 tbsp.	15 mL

Apricot Stuffing: Combine first 8 ingredients in medium bowl. Makes about 2 1/3 cups (575 mL) stuffing.

Loosely fill body cavity of chicken with stuffing. Secure with wooden picks or small metal skewers. Tie wings with butcher's string close to body. Tie legs to tail.

Soak wood chips in water for 20 minutes. Drain. Put chips in smoker box (see Note 3). Close smoker box. Place smoker box over 1 side of grill in gas barbecue. Heat barbecue to medium for about 20 minutes until chips are smoking. Adjust burner under smoker box as necessary to keep it smoking and to maintain temperature of about 350°F (175°C). Place a small piece of greased foil on grill opposite smoker box. Place chicken on foil. Turn off burner under chicken. Close lid. Cook for 1 3/4 hours.

(continued on next page)

Grilled Greats

Have a water spray bottle on hand to lightly douse any flames which may occur from wood chips in smoker box.

Combine remaining 4 ingredients in small bowl. Brush over chicken. Cook for about 15 minutes, brushing with soy sauce mixture, until chicken is fully cooked and meat thermometer inserted into thickest part of breast reads 180°F (83°C). Temperature of stuffing should reach at least 165°F (74°C). Transfer chicken to cutting board. Remove stuffing to serving bowl. Cover to keep warm. Cover chicken with foil. Let stand for 10 minutes before carving. Serves 6.

1 serving: 798 Calories; 52.8 g Total Fat (22.9 g Mono, 12.0 g Poly, 13.7 g Sat); 227 mg Cholesterol; 21 g Carbohydrate; 2 g Fibre; 58 g Protein; 708 mg Sodium

Note 1: If you are unable to find apricots in syrup in your local store, use sliced peaches instead.

Note 2: Wood chips for your barbecue can be found in the barbecue section of department stores or in barbecue specialty stores.

Note 3: If you do not own a smoker box, you can make your own using a foil pan. Fill the pan with the soaked wood chips and cover with a sheet of foil. Poke holes in the top to allow smoke to escape.

Paré Pointer

Why did the whale cross the ocean?
To get to the other tide.

Citrus Spice Chicken

The best zest in town! This'll freshen up any dinner table.

Orange juice	1/2 cup	125 mL
Lime juice	1/4 cup	60 mL
Balsamic vinegar	2 tbsp.	30 mL
Dijon mustard	1 tbsp.	15 mL
Finely chopped chipotle pepper in adobo sauce (see Tip)	1 tbsp.	15 mL
Garlic cloves, minced (or 1/2 tsp., 2 mL, powder)	2	2
Dried oregano	1 tsp.	5 mL
Chili powder	1/2 tsp.	2 mL
Ground cumin	1/4 tsp.	1 mL
Salt	1/4 tsp.	1 mL
Chicken legs, back attached (11 – 12 oz., 310 – 340 g, each)	4	4
Cooking oil	2 tbsp.	30 mL

Process first 10 ingredients in blender until smooth. Pour into large resealable freezer bag.

Add chicken. Seal bag. Turn until coated. Let stand in refrigerator for 2 hours, turning occasionally. Remove chicken. Transfer orange juice mixture to small saucepan. Bring to a boil. Reduce heat to medium-low. Simmer for at least 5 minutes. Set aside.

Pat chicken dry with paper towel. Brush both sides of chicken with cooking oil. Preheat gas barbecue to medium-high. Place chicken on one side of greased grill. Reduce heat on burner under chicken to low, leaving opposite burner on medium. Close lid. Cook for 30 minutes. Turn and brush generously with reserved orange juice mixture. Cook for another 25 minutes until internal temperature reaches 170°F (77°C). Brush with remaining orange juice mixture before serving. Makes 4 legs.

1 leg: 286 Calories; 15.5 g Total Fat (7.0 g Mono, 4.1 g Poly, 2.8 g Sat); 102 mg Cholesterol; 7 g Carbohydrate; 1 g Fibre; 28 g Protein; 302 mg Sodium

Pictured on front cover.

 Chipotle chili peppers are smoked jalapeno peppers. Be sure to wash your hands after handling. To store any leftover chipotle chili peppers, divide into recipe-friendly portions and freeze, with sauce, in airtight containers for up to one year.

Grilled Greats

Beer Can Chicken

Check the barbecue section of your local department store for a roasting stand that is specially made to hold the beer can and chicken safely.

Can of beer	12 1/2 oz.	355 mL
Apple juice	1/4 cup	60 mL
Apple cider vinegar	2 tbsp.	30 mL
Cooking oil	2 tbsp.	30 mL
Worcestershire sauce	2 tsp.	10 mL
Montreal chicken spice	2 tbsp.	30 mL
Brown sugar, packed	2 tsp.	10 mL
Dried oregano	1 tsp.	5 mL
Dry mustard	1 tsp.	5 mL
Onion powder	1 tsp.	5 mL
Whole chicken	4 lbs.	1.8 kg

Pour 2/3 cup (150 mL) beer into a spray bottle, leaving remaining beer in can. Set can aside. Add next 4 ingredients to spray bottle. Swirl gently to combine. Set aside.

Combine next 5 ingredients in small bowl.

Sprinkle 1 tbsp. (15 mL) seasoning mixture inside chicken cavity. Rub remaining seasoning mixture over surface of chicken. Let stand, covered, in refrigerator for 30 minutes. Stand the chicken, tail end down, over beer can and press down to insert can into body cavity of chicken. Preheat gas barbecue to medium. Place drip pan under grill on one side of barbecue. Balance chicken upright over drip pan, so that bottom of beer can rests on grill. Turn burner under chicken to low, leaving opposite burner on medium. Close lid. Cook for 1 1/2 to 1 3/4 hours, spraying chicken with beer mixture every 20 minutes, until browned and meat thermometer inserted in thickest part of breast reads 180°F (83°C). Carefully remove chicken from beer can by inserting a carving fork through chicken above level of top of beer can and lifting chicken off of can (see Note). Transfer chicken to cutting board. Cover with foil. Let stand for 10 minutes before carving. Serves 6.

1 serving: 754 Calories; 50.4 g Total Fat (21.6 g Mono, 11.1 g Poly, 13.4 g Sat); 227 mg Cholesterol; 10 g Carbohydrate; trace Fibre; 57 g Protein; 607 mg Sodium

Note: It is important to be very careful when removing the beer can from the chicken. The can will be full of very hot liquid.

Mediterranean Burgers

These Mediterranean burgers are far from mediocre.
Feta, onion, red pepper and a variety of herbs and spices
give these burgers an extraordinary amount of flavour!

Butter (or hard margarine)	1 1/2 tsp.	7 mL
Chopped onion	1 cup	250 mL
Roasted red peppers, drained and blotted dry, chopped	3/4 cup	175 mL
Red wine vinegar	2 tbsp.	30 mL
White bread slice, torn into small pieces	1	1
Lemon juice	2 tbsp.	30 mL
Grated lemon zest	2 tsp.	10 mL
Garlic clove, minced (or 1/4 tsp., 1 mL, powder)	1	1
Dried oregano	1 tsp.	5 mL
Dried thyme	1 tsp.	5 mL
Seasoned salt	1 tsp.	5 mL
Pepper	1/2 tsp.	2 mL
Lean ground chicken	1 1/2 lbs.	680 g
Crumbled feta cheese	1/2 cup	125 mL
Cream cheese, softened	1/4 cup	60 mL
Hamburger buns, split	6	6

Melt butter in large frying pan on medium. Add onion. Cook for 5 to 10 minutes, stirring often, until softened.

Add red pepper and vinegar. Stir. Reduce heat to medium-low. Cook for about 15 minutes, stirring occasionally, until onion is very soft. Remove from heat. Cover to keep warm.

Put bread and lemon juice into medium bowl. Stir until bread is moistened. Add next 6 ingredients. Stir.

Add chicken. Mix well. Divide into 6 equal portions. Shape into 4 1/2 inch (11 cm) diameter patties.

Put feta and cream cheese into small bowl. Mash until smooth. Preheat gas barbecue to medium (see Tip, page 21).

(continued on next page)

Cook patties on greased grill for 6 to 8 minutes per side until fully cooked and internal temperature reaches 175°F (80°C). Spread cheese mixture on top of patties. Cook for about 1 minute until cheese is softened. Remove to plate. Cover to keep warm.

Toast bun halves on greased grill for about 1 minute until golden. Serve patties, topped with onion mixture, in buns. Makes 6 burgers.

1 burger: 486 Calories; 24.4 g Total Fat (2.3 g Mono, 1.2 g Poly, 5.2 g Sat); 25 mg Cholesterol; 34 g Carbohydrate; 2 g Fibre; 28 g Protein; 1050 mg Sodium

Variation: Use 3/4 cup (175 mL) goat cheese in place of feta and cream cheese.

Sesame Ginger Chicken

Ginger and sesame mingle magnificently in the marvellous marinade.

Soy sauce	1/3 cup	75 mL
Rice vinegar	3 tbsp.	50 mL
Sesame oil	3 tbsp.	50 mL
Brown sugar, packed	2 tbsp.	30 mL
Finely grated gingerroot (or 3/4 tsp., 4 mL, ground ginger)	1 tbsp.	15 mL
Garlic cloves, minced (or 1/2 tsp., 2 mL, powder)	2	2
Boneless, skinless chicken breast halves (4 – 6 oz., 113 – 170 g, each)	4	4
Sesame seeds, toasted (see Tip, page 13)	1 tbsp.	15 mL

Combine first 6 ingredients in large resealable freezer bag.

Add chicken. Seal bag. Turn until coated. Let stand in refrigerator for at least 6 hours or overnight, turning occasionally. Remove chicken. Transfer soy sauce mixture to small saucepan. Bring to a boil. Reduce heat to medium. Boil gently, uncovered, for at least 5 minutes, until thickened and reduced by half.

Preheat gas barbecue to medium (see Tip, page 21). Cook chicken on greased grill for 15 to 17 minutes, turning occasionally and brushing with reserved soy sauce mixture, until fully cooked and internal temperature reaches 170°F (77°C).

Sprinkle with sesame seeds. Serves 4.

1 breast: 271 Calories; 13.0 g Total Fat (4.9 g Mono, 5.1 g Poly, 2.1 g Sat); 66 mg Cholesterol; 10 g Carbohydrate; trace Fibre; 28 g Protein; 1735 mg Sodium

Grilled Greats

Cedar Plank Chicken

Wow and amaze your friends with the delicious novelty of serving dinner on an aromatic plank. They won't believe how moist and delicious chicken can be with a little help from a cedar! (Keep in mind that long soaking and marinating times are required.)

Cedar plank (see Note)	1	1
Red jalapeño jelly	1/2 cup	125 mL
Italian dressing	1/2 cup	125 mL
Grated orange zest	2 tbsp.	30 mL
Bone-in chicken breast halves (10 – 11 oz., 285 – 310 g, each)	4	4
Brown sugar, packed	1 tbsp.	15 mL
Dried sage	1/2 tsp.	2 mL
Paprika	1/2 tsp.	2 mL
Salt	1/2 tsp.	2 mL
Pepper	1/2 tsp.	2 mL
Cooking oil	1 tbsp.	15 mL

Place cedar plank in sink or large container. Add enough water to cover. Weight planks with heavy cans to keep submerged. Let stand for at least 6 hours or overnight.

Put jalapeño jelly in small microwave-safe bowl. Microwave on high (100%) for about 1 minute until melted. Add dressing and orange zest. Stir. Pour into large resealable freezer bag.

Add chicken. Seal bag. Turn until coated. Let stand in refrigerator for 4 to 6 hours, turning occasionally. Remove chicken. Discard any remaining dressing mixture.

Combine next 5 ingredients in small cup. Rub on both sides of chicken.

Brush cooking oil on one side of plank. Arrange chicken, skin-side up, on greased side of plank. Preheat gas barbecue to medium. Place plank on ungreased grill. Close lid. Cook for about 50 minutes until chicken is fully cooked and internal temperature reaches 170°F (77°C). Serves 4 lucky people.

1 breast: 331 Calories; 13.6 g Total Fat (6.6 g Mono, 3.9 g Poly, 2.0 g Sat); 119 mg Cholesterol; 9 g Carbohydrate; trace Fibre; 41 g Protein; 515 mg Sodium

Pictured on page 36.

(continued on next page)

Grilled Greats

Note: Cedar planks specifically designed for barbecuing can be purchased in the meat department of large grocery stores. Or use an untreated western red cedar plank found in building supply stores. Never use a treated cedar plank. Planks should be about 16 × 6 × 1/2 inches (40 × 15 × 1.2 cm) and are good for 1 use each.

Chicken Aztec

We know that Aztec life was anything but tranquil, but you've got to pay homage to a culture that used chocolate for currency! Savour the secrets of the Ancients and taste the mysterious, dark accents chocolate and cocoa provide when paired with chicken.

Cooking oil	1 tbsp.	15 mL
Brown sugar, packed	2 tsp.	10 mL
Lime juice	2 tsp.	10 mL
Chili powder	1 tsp.	5 mL
Cocoa	1 tsp.	5 mL
Ground cinnamon	1 tsp.	5 mL
Boneless, skinless chicken breast halves (4 – 6 oz., 113 – 170 g, each)	4	4
Melted butter (or hard margarine)	3 tbsp.	50 mL
Chopped fresh cilantro or parsley	2 tbsp.	30 mL
Finely chopped green onion	1 tbsp.	15 mL
Lime juice	1 tbsp.	15 mL
Finely diced jalapeño pepper (see Tip, page 33)	1 tsp.	5 mL
Grated semi-sweet chocolate	1 tsp.	5 mL

Combine first 6 ingredients in small bowl.

Brush on both sides of chicken. Preheat gas barbecue to medium (see Tip, page 21). Cook chicken on greased grill for about 10 minutes per side until fully cooked and internal temperature reaches 170°F (77°C). Remove to serving plate. Cover to keep warm.

Combine remaining 6 ingredients in small bowl. Spoon over chicken. Serves 4.

1 serving: 254 Calories; 14.3 g Total Fat (4.8 g Mono, 1.8 g Poly, 6.4 g Sat); 88 mg Cholesterol; 5 g Carbohydrate; 1 g Fibre; 26 g Protein; 133 mg Sodium

Pictured on page 36.

Greek Lemon Pitas

*Lemon lovers, this pita's for you! Lots of lemon flavour in a warm
pita pocket filled with all sorts of tasty ingredients.*

Lemon juice	1/4 cup	60 mL
Liquid honey	3 tbsp.	50 mL
Garlic clove, minced (or 1/4 tsp., 1 mL, powder)	1	1
Dried oregano	1 tsp.	5 mL
Pepper	1/4 tsp.	1 mL
Boneless, skinless chicken thighs, quartered (about 3 oz, 85 g, each)	8	8
Seasoned salt	1/2 tsp.	2 mL
Bamboo skewers (8 inches, 20 cm, each) soaked in water for 10 minutes	8	8
Thin lemon slices (about 1/2 lemon)	8	8
Salt	1/2 tsp.	2 mL
Plain yogurt	1 cup	250 mL
Chopped Kalamata (or black) olives	1/2 cup	125 mL
Liquid honey	2 tbsp.	30 mL
Chopped fresh parsley (or 3/4 tsp., 4 mL, flakes)	1 tbsp.	15 mL
Chopped fresh mint (or 3/4 tsp., 4 mL, dried)	1 tbsp.	15 mL
Shredded romaine lettuce, lightly packed	2 cups	500 mL
Pita bread (7 inch, 18 cm, diameter), halved and opened	4	4

Combine first 5 ingredients in medium bowl.

Add chicken. Stir until coated. Let stand at room temperature for
20 minutes. Drain and discard lemon juice mixture.

Sprinkle chicken with seasoned salt. Thread onto skewers. Fold lemon
slices into quarters and thread onto ends of skewers. Preheat gas barbecue
to medium (see Tip, page 21). Cook skewers on greased grill for about
15 minutes, turning occasionally, until chicken is no longer pink inside.
Remove lemon slices to cutting board. Remove chicken from skewers.
Cover to keep warm. Finely chop lemon. Sprinkle with salt.

(continued on next page)

Grilled Greats

Combine next 5 ingredients in medium bowl. Add lemon. Stir. Add lettuce and chicken. Toss.

Place pita pockets on warm grill. Heat for 30 seconds. Fill pockets with chicken mixture. Makes 8 pockets.

1 pocket: 265 Calories; 8.7 g Total Fat (3.4 g Mono, 1.7 g Poly, 2.6 g Sat); 60 mg Cholesterol; 27 g Carbohydrate; 1 g Fibre; 19 g Protein; 474 mg Sodium

Grilled Hoisin Drumsticks

No hoisin around—these slowly marinated drumsticks are just too good! The caramelized hoisin glaze is so sweet and, dare we say, scandalously sticky, that you'll want to have a napkin or 2 at the ready.

Cooking oil	1/3 cup	75 mL
Rice wine (or dry sherry)	3 tbsp.	50 mL
Garlic cloves, minced	3	3
Finely grated gingerroot	1 tsp.	5 mL
Chicken drumsticks (3 – 5 oz., 85 – 140 g, each)	12	12
Brown sugar, packed	2/3 cup	150 mL
Soy sauce	1/2 cup	125 mL
Hoisin sauce	1/3 cup	75 mL
Ketchup	1/3 cup	75 mL

Combine first 4 ingredients in large resealable freezer bag.

Add chicken. Seal bag. Turn until coated. Let stand in refrigerator for 6 hours or overnight, turning occasionally. Remove chicken. Discard any remaining cooking oil mixture.

Combine remaining 4 ingredients in small bowl. Preheat gas barbecue to medium (see Tip, page 21). Cook chicken on greased grill for 25 minutes, turning occasionally. Brush with soy sauce mixture. Cook for another 15 minutes, turning often and brushing with soy sauce mixture, until fully cooked and internal temperature reaches 170°F (77°C). Makes 12 drumsticks.

1 drumstick: 195 Calories; 6.0 g Total Fat (2.3 g Mono, 1.6 g Poly, 1.3 g Sat); 66 mg Cholesterol; 17.3 g Carbohydrate; trace Fibre; 18 g Protein; 1189 mg Sodium

Pictured on page 53.

Minted Cider Chicken

A hint of mint adds a touch of spring to this mildly sweet, glazed chicken.

Finely chopped fresh mint	1/4 cup	60 mL
Red jalapeño jelly, melted	1/4 cup	60 mL
Apple cider vinegar	2 tbsp.	30 mL
Frozen concentrated apple juice, thawed	1 tbsp.	15 mL
Garlic clove, minced (or 1/4 tsp., 1 mL, powder)	1	1
Salt	1/4 tsp.	1 mL
Pepper	1/8 tsp.	0.5 mL
Chicken drumsticks (or bone-in thighs) (3 – 5 oz., 85 – 140 g, each)	12	12

Combine first 7 ingredients in small bowl.

Preheat gas barbecue to medium-high (see Tip, page 21). Cook chicken on greased grill for about 30 minutes, turning occasionally, until starting to brown. Brush with mint mixture. Cook for another 15 minutes, turning occasionally and brushing with mint mixture, until fully cooked and internal temperature reaches 170°F (77°C). Makes 12 drumsticks.

1 drumstick: 75 Calories; 2.0 g Total Fat (0.7 g Mono, 0.5 g Poly, 0.5 g Sat); 32 mg Cholesterol; 4 g Carbohydrate; trace Fibre; 10 g Protein; 82 mg Sodium

1. Sunday Fried Chicken, page 80
2. Grilled Hoisin Drumsticks, page 51
3. Italian Burgers, page 74

Props courtesy of: Pier 1 Imports
Dansk Gifts
Danesco Inc.
Emile Henry

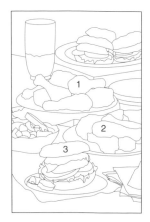

Fridge Door Chicken

This simple recipe is flavoured entirely with ingredients conveniently found in your fridge door. A little of this, a little of that and everyone will be saying, "Wow, you've got great legs!" (To keep your legs looking their best, remember to factor in the long marinating time.)

Ketchup	1/2 cup	125 mL
Raspberry jam	1/4 cup	60 mL
Chopped chipotle pepper in adobo sauce (see Tip, page 44)	1 tbsp.	15 mL
Dijon mustard	1 tbsp.	15 mL
Steak sauce	1 tbsp.	15 mL
Chicken drumsticks (3 – 5 oz., 85 – 140 g, each)	12	12

Whisk first 5 ingredients in small bowl.

Put chicken in large resealable freezer bag. Add ketchup mixture. Seal bag. Turn until coated. Let stand in refrigerator for at least 6 hours or overnight, turning occasionally. Remove chicken. Transfer ketchup mixture to small saucepan. Bring to a boil. Reduce heat to medium. Boil gently, uncovered, for at least 5 minutes, stirring often. Preheat gas barbecue to medium-high. Place chicken on one side of greased grill. Turn burner under chicken to low, leaving opposite burner on medium-high. Close lid. Cook for about 1 hour, turning often and brushing with reserved ketchup mixture, until fully cooked and internal temperature reaches 170°F (77°C). Makes 12 drumsticks.

1 drumstick: 137 Calories; 4.4 g Total Fat (1.4 g Mono, 1.1 g Poly, 1.1 g Sat); 65 mg Cholesterol; 7 g Carbohydrate; trace Fibre; 16 g Protein; 227 mg Sodium

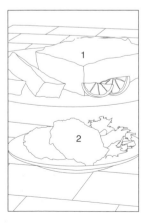

1. Chipotle Chicken Loaf, page 61
2. Chili-Rubbed Chicken, page 69

Props courtesy of: Danesco Inc.

Chicken Peanut Satay

This sweet satay does double duty as an entree or a party-pleasing appie.
The dipping sauce is similar to Thai peanut sauce but is a little milder.

Cooking oil	2 tbsp.	30 mL
Sesame oil (for flavour)	2 tsp.	10 mL
Garlic clove, minced (or 1/4 tsp., 1 mL, powder)	1	1
Finely grated gingerroot (or 1/4 tsp., 1 mL, ground ginger)	1 tsp.	5 mL
Dried crushed chilies	1/2 tsp.	2 mL
Grated lime zest	1/2 tsp.	2 mL
Ground coriander	1/2 tsp.	2 mL
Ground turmeric	1/2 tsp.	2 mL
Chicken breast fillets (see Note)	1 1/2 lbs.	680 g
Bamboo skewers (8 inches, 20 cm, each), soaked in water for 10 minutes	12	12
Salt, sprinkle		
Pepper, sprinkle		
SATAY PEANUT SAUCE		
Light coconut milk	1 cup	250 mL
Chunky peanut butter	1/2 cup	125 mL
Brown sugar, packed	1 tbsp.	15 mL
Lime juice	1 tbsp.	15 mL
Fish sauce	2 tsp.	10 mL
Rice vinegar	2 tsp.	10 mL
Dried crushed chilies	1/2 tsp.	2 mL

Combine first 8 ingredients in medium bowl.

Add chicken. Stir until coated. Let stand, covered, in refrigerator for at least 1 hour, or up to 24 hours.

Thread chicken onto skewers, accordion-style. Discard any remaining seasoning mixture. Sprinkle with salt and pepper. Preheat gas barbecue to medium (see Tip, page 21). Cook on greased grill for 3 to 4 minutes per side until no longer pink inside. Remove to serving plate.

(continued on next page)

Satay Peanut Sauce: Combine all 7 ingredients in small saucepan on medium. Bring to a boil. Reduce heat to medium-low. Simmer, uncovered, for 3 to 5 minutes, stirring occasionally, until the consistency of thick gravy. Makes about 1 1/3 cups (325 mL) sauce. Serve with satays. Makes 12 satays.

1 satay with 1 1/2 tbsp. (25 mL) sauce: 159 Calories; 9.2 g Total Fat (3.9 g Mono, 2.3 g Poly, 2.2 g Sat); 33 mg Cholesterol; 4 g Carbohydrate; 1 g Fibre; 16 g Protein; 160 mg Sodium

Note: Chicken breast halves may be used instead of chicken fillets. Cut breasts lengthwise into 1/4 inch (6 mm) thick strips.

Orange Basil Chicken

This juicy dish is spatchcocked—meaning cut open and pressed flat before it's grilled. Use kitchen shears to make the job easy.

Butter (or hard margarine), softened	3 tbsp.	50 mL
Chopped fresh basil	2 tbsp.	30 mL
Grated orange zest	1 tsp.	5 mL
Ground cumin	1/2 tsp.	2 mL
Salt	1/4 tsp.	1 mL
Pepper	1/4 tsp.	1 mL
Whole chicken	4 – 4 1/2 lbs.	1.8 – 2 kg
Frozen concentrated orange juice, thawed	2 tbsp.	30 mL
Maple (or maple-flavoured) syrup	2 tbsp.	30 mL

Combine first 6 ingredients in small bowl.

Place chicken, backbone up, on cutting board. Cut down both sides of backbone, using kitchen shears or knife, to remove. Turn chicken over. Press chicken flat. Carefully loosen skin but do not remove (see Note). Stuff butter mixture between meat and skin, spreading mixture as evenly as possible. Preheat gas barbecue to medium. Place chicken, skin-side down, on 1 side of greased grill. Turn off burner under chicken, leaving opposite burner on medium. Close lid. Cook for 45 minutes. Carefully turn chicken over.

Combine concentrated orange juice and maple syrup in small cup. Brush over chicken. Cook for another 30 minutes, brushing occasionally with orange juice mixture, until meat thermometer inserted into thickest part of breast reads 180°F (83°C). Transfer chicken to cutting board. Cover with foil. Let stand for 15 minutes before carving. Serves 6.

1 serving: 728 Calories; 51.3 g Total Fat (20.4 g Mono, 10.0 g Poly, 16.6 g Sat); 242 mg Cholesterol; 7 g Carbohydrate; trace Fibre; 57 g Protein; 351 mg Sodium

Note: To loosen chicken skin, lift edge of skin and gently slide fingers as far as possible underneath skin. Be careful not to tear the skin.

Uptown Asparagus Chicken

We know you can forget all your troubles, forget all your cares downtown, but when it comes to chicken, things will be great uptown. The delightful presentation and the combination of havarti, asparagus and ham over lemon-peppered chicken is well worth the change of location.

Fresh asparagus, trimmed of tough ends	1 lb.	454 g
Boneless, skinless chicken breast halves (4 – 6 oz., 113 – 170 g, each)	4	4
Cooking oil	1 tbsp.	15 mL
Lemon pepper	1/2 tsp.	2 mL
Thin deli ham slices (about 4 oz., 113 g)	4	4
Roasted red peppers, drained and blotted dry, cut into strips	1/2 cup	125 mL
Slices of havarti cheese, cut diagonally into triangles (about 4 oz., 113 g)	4	4

Blanch asparagus in boiling salted water in medium frying pan for about 2 minutes until bright green. Drain. Immediately plunge into ice water in large bowl. Let stand for 5 minutes. Drain well.

Place 1 chicken breast between 2 sheets of plastic wrap. Pound with mallet or rolling pin to 1/2 inch (12 mm) thickness. Transfer to greased baking sheet with sides. Repeat with remaining chicken. Brush chicken with cooking oil. Sprinkle with lemon pepper. Broil on top rack in oven for about 7 minutes until golden brown and internal temperature reaches 170°F (77°C).

Place 1 slice of ham, folding if necessary, on each chicken breast. Place 3 or 4 asparagus spears over ham. Arrange red pepper strips over asparagus. Overlap 2 triangles of cheese over red pepper. Broil for about 2 minutes until cheese is melted and bubbling. Serves 4.

1 serving: 362 Calories; 14.9 g Total Fat (2.5 g Mono, 1.5 g Poly, 6.9 g Sat); 104 mg Cholesterol; 12 g Carbohydrate; 2 g Fibre; 42 g Protein; 973 mg Sodium

Pictured on page 90.

Biscuit-Topped Chili

*Put some heat into what you eat with this salsa-flavoured chili treat—
topped off with golden biscuits! Make it a complete meal by adding
a side salad. Make it a party by adding a margarita!*

Cooking oil	1 tbsp.	15 mL
Lean ground chicken	1 lb.	454 g
Chopped onion	1/4 cup	60 mL
Can of red kidney beans, rinsed and drained	14 oz.	398 mL
Salsa	1 1/2 cups	375 mL
Can of condensed tomato soup	10 oz.	284 mL
All-purpose flour	2 cups	500 mL
Baking powder	1 tbsp.	15 mL
Granulated sugar	2 tsp.	10 mL
Seasoned salt	1 tsp.	5 mL
Pepper	1/4 tsp.	1 mL
Milk	2/3 cup	150 mL
Cooking oil	1/3 cup	75 mL

Heat first amount of cooking oil in large frying pan on medium-high.
Add chicken and onion. Scramble-fry for about 8 minutes until chicken
is starting to brown and onion is softened.

Add next 3 ingredients. Cook and stir until heated through. Transfer to
greased 9 inch (22 cm) deep dish pie plate.

Measure next 5 ingredients into medium bowl. Stir. Make a well in centre.

Add milk and second amount of cooking oil to well. Stir until just moistened.
Turn dough out onto lightly floured surface. Knead 8 times. Roll or pat
dough to 9 inch (22 cm) diameter circle. Place over chicken mixture.
Prick entire surface of dough with fork through to bottom of pan. Bake,
uncovered, in 400°F (205°C) oven for 25 to 30 minutes until golden.
Serves 4.

*1 serving: 859 Calories; 38.5 g Total Fat (12.6 g Mono, 6.9 g Poly, 2.0 g Sat); 2 mg Cholesterol;
90 g Carbohydrate; 11 g Fibre; 36 g Protein; 1403 mg Sodium*

Coconut Curry Casserole

Creamy, dreamy and loaded with sweet coconut and curry flavours, consider this dish to be la crème de la crème of casseroles.

Large egg, fork-beaten	1	1
Cooked long grain white rice (about 1 cup, 250 mL, uncooked), see Note	3 cups	750 mL
Crushed unsalted peanuts	1/4 cup	60 mL
Salt	1/2 tsp.	2 mL
Pepper	1/2 tsp.	2 mL
Brown sugar, packed	3 tbsp.	50 mL
All-purpose flour	1 tbsp.	15 mL
Can of coconut milk	14 oz.	398 mL
Soy sauce	3 tbsp.	50 mL
Lime juice	2 tbsp.	30 mL
Red curry paste	1/2 tsp.	2 mL
Cooking oil	1 tbsp.	15 mL
Boneless, skinless chicken breast halves, cut into 1 inch (2.5 cm) cubes	1 lb.	454 g
Can of cut baby corn, drained	14 oz.	398 mL
Chopped fresh asparagus, trimmed of tough ends	1 cup	250 mL
Chopped red pepper	1 cup	250 mL

Combine first 5 ingredients in large bowl. Press rice mixture evenly into bottom of greased 2 quart (2 L) shallow baking dish. Bake in 350°F (175°C) oven for about 15 minutes until golden. Set aside.

Combine brown sugar and flour in medium bowl. Add next 4 ingredients. Stir until smooth.

Heat cooking oil in large frying pan on medium-high. Add chicken. Cook for about 5 minutes, stirring occasionally, until browned. Remove to small bowl. Reduce heat to medium. Add coconut milk mixture. Heat and stir for about 3 minutes until boiling and thickened.

Add remaining 3 ingredients and chicken. Stir. Spoon over rice mixture in baking dish. Bake, uncovered, in 350°F (175°C) oven for about 25 minutes until chicken is tender and vegetables are tender-crisp. Let stand for 5 minutes before serving. Serves 4.

(continued on next page)

1 serving: 757 Calories; 34.1 g Total Fat (6.6 g Mono, 4.0 g Poly, 20.9 g Sat); 112 mg Cholesterol; 80 g Carbohydrate; 5.2 g Fibre; 40 g Protein; 1426 mg Sodium

Pictured on page 71 and back cover.

Note: For best results, use rice that is cooled to room temperature.

Chipotle Chicken Loaf

By using convenient pre-shredded cheese, jarred salsa and bagged bread crumbs, this family-friendly meatloaf will give you more time to loaf around!

Large egg, fork-beaten	1	1
Finely chopped onion	1 1/2 cups	375 mL
Grated Mexican cheese blend	1 cup	250 mL
Fine dry bread crumbs	1/2 cup	125 mL
Salsa	1/2 cup	125 mL
Garlic cloves, minced (or 1/2 tsp., 2 mL, powder)	2	2
Chili powder	1 tsp.	5 mL
Finely chopped chipotle pepper in adobo sauce (see Tip, page 44)	1 tsp.	5 mL
Salt	1/2 tsp.	2 mL
Pepper	1/4 tsp	1 mL
Lean ground chicken	2 lbs.	900 g
Grated Mexican cheese blend	1/2 cup	125 mL
Lime wedges, for garnish		

Combine first 10 ingredients in large bowl.

Add chicken. Mix well. Press into greased 9 × 5 × 3 inch (22 × 12.5 × 7.5 cm) loaf pan. Bake, uncovered, in 350°F (175°C) oven for 30 minutes.

Sprinkle second amount of cheese evenly over loaf. Bake for another 45 to 50 minutes until fully cooked and internal temperature reaches 175°F (80°C). Let stand for 10 minutes. Cut into slices.

Garnish individual servings with lime wedges. Serves 8.

1 serving: 359 Calories; 23.1 g Total Fat (0.5 g Mono, 0.2 g Poly, 4.8 g Sat); 42 mg Cholesterol; 10 g Carbohydrate; 1 g Fibre; 26 g Protein; 499 mg Sodium

Pictured on page 54.

Lemon Basil Chicken Rolls

Roll out the red carpet in honour of these exquisite chicken rolls.
Your guests will think you've been slaving in the kitchen
all day—even though they're actually quite simple to make!

Fine dry bread crumbs	1/4 cup	60 mL
Basil pesto	2 tbsp.	30 mL
Grated lemon zest	1 tsp.	5 mL
Boneless, skinless chicken breast halves (4 – 6 oz., 113 – 170 g, each)	4	4
Large egg	1	1
Water	1 tbsp.	15 mL
Fine dry bread crumbs	3/4 cup	175 mL
Paprika	1 tsp.	5 mL
Salt	1/2 tsp.	2 mL
Pepper	1/4 tsp.	1 mL
Chopped fresh basil, for garnish		

Combine first 3 ingredients in small cup.

Place 1 chicken breast between 2 sheets of plastic wrap. Pound with mallet or rolling pin to 1/2 inch (12 mm) thickness. Spread pesto mixture over chicken, leaving about 1/2 inch (12 mm) edge. Roll up tightly, jelly-roll style. Secure with wooden pick. Repeat with remaining chicken and pesto mixture.

Beat egg and water with fork in small bowl.

Combine next 4 ingredients in small shallow dish. Dip chicken rolls into egg mixture. Press into crumb mixture until coated. Place on greased baking sheet with sides. Discard any remaining egg and crumb mixtures. Bake in 400°F (205°C) oven for 25 to 30 minutes until fully cooked and internal temperature reaches 170°F (77°C). Remove wooden picks. Slice rolls in half diagonally to serve.

Garnish with basil. Makes 4 rolls.

1 roll: 268 Calories; 7.9 g Total Fat (1.4 g Mono, 0.8 g Poly, 1.7 g Sat); 103 mg Cholesterol; 16 g Carbohydrate; 1 g Fibre; 31 g Protein; 506 mg Sodium

Pictured on page 90.

Savoury Bread Pudding

If stuffing sends you sailing over the moon with delight, this delicious strata will send you clear to another galaxy. Truly out of this world!

White (or whole wheat) bread cubes	3 cups	750 mL
Diced onion	1 cup	250 mL
Chicken (or turkey) sausages, cut into 1/2 inch (12 mm) pieces (about 3 oz., 85 g)	3	3
Bacon slices, diced	3	3
Boneless, skinless chicken breast halves, cut into 3/4 inch (2 cm) cubes	1/2 lb.	225 g
Large eggs	6	6
Milk	1 1/4 cups	300 mL
Italian seasoning	1 1/2 tsp	7 mL
Salt	1/2 tsp	2 mL
Pepper	1/2 tsp	2 mL
Grated medium Cheddar cheese	1 1/2 cups	375 mL
Grated Parmesan cheese	1/2 cup	125 mL

Arrange bread cubes in single layer on ungreased baking sheet with sides. Bake in 350°F (175°C) oven for 10 to 12 minutes until toasted. Cool.

Cook next 3 ingredients in large frying pan on medium for about 15 minutes, stirring often, until bacon is crisp and onion and sausage are browned. Transfer with slotted spoon to paper towel-lined plate to drain. Increase heat to medium-high.

Add chicken to same frying pan. Cook for 1 minute, stirring constantly. Remove to separate plate.

Whisk next 5 ingredients in large bowl until smooth. Add bread cubes. Stir. Let stand for 10 minutes to allow bread to absorb egg mixture. Add chicken and bacon mixture. Stir. Spread evenly in greased 2 quart (2 L) shallow baking dish.

Sprinkle with both cheeses. Bake, uncovered, in 350°F (175°C) oven for about 40 minutes until top is browned and knife inserted in centre comes out clean. Serves 4.

1 serving: 586 Calories; 32.3 g Total Fat (10.4 g Mono, 2.7 g Poly, 16.6 g Sat); 390 mg Cholesterol; 23 g Carbohydrate; 1 g Fibre; 49 g Protein; 1277 mg Sodium

Picadillo Pastries

Packets of poultry poetry—feel free to reheat in the microwave.

Cooking oil	1 tbsp.	15 mL
Lean ground chicken	3/4 lb.	340 g
Salt	1/4 tsp.	1 mL
Chopped onion	2 cups	500 mL
Garlic clove, minced (or 1/4 tsp., 1 mL, powder)	1	1
Can of tomato sauce	7 1/2 oz.	213 mL
Chopped pimiento-stuffed olives	1/4 cup	60 mL
Chopped raisins	1/4 cup	60 mL
Lime juice	2 tbsp.	30 mL
Finely chopped chipotle pepper in adobo sauce (see Tip, page 44)	2 tsp.	10 mL
Chili powder	1 tsp.	5 mL
Dried oregano	1/2 tsp.	2 mL
Ground cinnamon	1/4 tsp.	1 mL
PASTRY		
Biscuit mix	4 1/2 cups	1.1 L
Finely chopped black olives (optional)	1/4 cup	60 mL
Boiling water	1 1/4 cups	300 mL
Milk	2 tbsp.	30 mL

Heat cooking oil in large frying pan on medium. Add chicken and salt. Scramble fry for about 5 minutes until chicken is no longer pink. Add onion and garlic. Cook for about 15 minutes, stirring often, until onion is browned.

Add next 8 ingredients. Cook for 1 minute, stirring constantly, to blend flavours. Remove from heat. Cool to room temperature.

Pastry: Combine biscuit mix and olives in medium bowl. Add boiling water. Stir until soft dough forms. Turn dough out onto lightly floured surface. Knead about 20 times until dough is smooth. Divide into 6 equal portions. Roll out 1 portion to form a 7 inch (18 cm) diameter circle. Place about 1/2 cup (125 mL) chicken mixture on half of circle, leaving 1/2 inch (12 mm) edge. Dampen edges of dough with water. Fold dough in half over filling. Crimp edges with fork to seal. Carefully transfer to greased baking sheet. Cut 2 small slits in top to allow steam to escape. Repeat with remaining dough portions and chicken mixture. Brush milk over pastries. Bake in 400°F (205°C) oven for about 30 minutes until golden brown. Makes 6 pastries.

(continued on next page)

1 pastry: 585 Calories; 25.0 g Total Fat (9.8 g Mono, 2.7 g Poly, 3.9 g Sat); 2 mg Cholesterol; 72 g Carbohydrate; 4 g Fibre; 19 g Protein; 1676 mg Sodium

Pictured on page 72.

Festive Chicken Bake

Enjoy the festive flavours of cranberry, orange, and cinnamon— any time of year! And be sure to make merry with all the time you save on prep. The sauce goes great with rice or noodles.

All-purpose flour	3 tbsp.	50 mL
Salt	1/4 tsp.	1 mL
Pepper	1/8 tsp.	0.5 mL
Paprika	1/8 tsp.	0.5 mL
Boneless, skinless chicken breast halves (4 – 6 oz., 113 – 170 g, each)	6	6
Cooking oil	1 tbsp.	15 mL
Prepared chicken broth	1/2 cup	125 mL
Frozen (or fresh) cranberries	1 cup	250 mL
Frozen concentrated orange juice, thawed	1/3 cup	75 mL
Diced onion	1/4 cup	60 mL
Ground cinnamon	1/4 tsp.	1 mL
Ground ginger	1/4 tsp.	1 mL

Combine first 4 ingredients in large resealable freezer bag. Add chicken. Toss until coated. Remove chicken. Reserve remaining flour mixture.

Heat cooking oil in large frying pan on medium-high. Add chicken. Cook for 2 to 3 minutes per side until browned. Arrange in single layer in greased 2 quart (2 L) shallow baking dish.

Stir broth into reserved flour mixture in small bowl until smooth. Add remaining 5 ingredients. Stir. Pour over chicken. Bake, covered, in 350°F (175°C) oven for about 45 minutes until fully cooked and internal temperature of chicken reaches 170°F (77°C). Serves 6.

1 serving: 199 Calories; 4.3 g Total Fat (1.9 g Mono, 1.2 g Poly, 0.7 g Sat); 66 mg Cholesterol; 12 g Carbohydrate; 1 g Fibre; 27 g Protein; 226 mg Sodium

Pictured on page 90.

Fennel Roast Chicken

Not your everyday roast chicken. Take the usual Sunday night fare up a notch with this dressy and flavourful fennel, sausage and wild rice stuffing.

SAUSAGE FENNEL STUFFING		
Water	2 1/4 cups	550 mL
Package of long grain and wild rice mix	6 1/4 oz.	180 g
Chopped sun-dried tomatoes	1/2 cup	125 mL
Fennel seed	1 tsp.	5 mL
Mild Italian sausages, casing removed and chopped	2	2
Olive oil	1 tsp.	5 mL
Chopped onion	1 cup	250 mL
Finely chopped fennel bulb (white part only)	1 cup	250 mL
Whole chicken	5 – 6 lbs.	2.3 – 2.7 kg
Olive oil	1 tbsp.	15 mL
Dried sage	2 tsp.	10 mL
Dried thyme	2 tsp.	10 mL
Lemon pepper	1 1/2 tsp.	7 mL
Fennel seed, crushed (see Note)	1 tsp.	5 mL
Olive oil	1 tbsp.	15 mL
Thickly sliced fennel bulb (white part only)	5 cups	1.25 L
Garlic cloves, minced	4	4
Dry (or alcohol-free) white wine	1/2 cup	125 mL
Prepared chicken broth	1/2 cup	125 mL

Chopped fresh sage, for garnish
Chopped fresh thyme, for garnish

Sausage Fennel Stuffing: Combine first 4 ingredients in medium saucepan. Bring to a boil. Reduce heat to medium-low. Cook, covered, for 20 to 25 minutes, without stirring, until rice is tender. Transfer to large bowl. Cool slightly. Fluff with fork.

Put sausage into medium frying pan. Scramble-fry on medium for about 5 minutes until no longer pink. Transfer sausage with slotted spoon to paper towel-lined plate to drain. Drain and discard drippings from pan.

(continued on next page)

Oven Ovations

Heat first amount of olive oil in same frying pan on medium. Add onion and first amount of fennel. Cook for about 5 minutes, stirring occasionally, until fennel is tender-crisp. Add to rice mixture. Add sausage. Stir. Makes about 5 cups (1.25 L) stuffing.

Loosely fill body cavity of chicken with stuffing. Secure with wooden picks or small metal skewers. Tie wings with butcher's string close to body. Tie legs to tail. Transfer to medium roasting pan.

Rub second amount of olive oil over surface of chicken. Combine next 4 ingredients in small cup. Sprinkle half of seasoning mixture over chicken. Bake, covered, in 400°F (205°C) oven for 20 minutes. Reduce heat to 350°F (175°C).

Combine next 3 ingredients and remaining seasoning mixture in large bowl. Arrange around chicken in roasting pan. Bake, uncovered, for 1 hour.

Pour wine and broth over chicken. Bake, uncovered, for another 30 to 40 minutes until meat thermometer inserted into thickest part of breast reads 180°F (83°C). Temperature of stuffing should reach at least 165°F (74°C). Remove chicken from oven. Remove stuffing to serving dish. Cover to keep warm. Cover chicken with foil. Let stand for 10 minutes before carving. Spoon vegetables and skimmed pan juices over chicken.

Garnish with sage and thyme. Serves 8.

1 serving: 762 Calories; 28 g Total Fat (12.2 g Mono, 5.3 g Poly, 7.3 g Sat); 226 mg Cholesterol; 43 g Carbohydrate; 10.4 g Fibre; 81 g Protein; 962 mg Sodium

Note: If you don't have a mortar and pestle, crush fennel seed on a cutting board using the flat side of a chef's knife.

Pictured on page 108.

Paré Pointer

Susie knew she shouldn't go in the water on a full stomach—
so she decided to swim on her back.

Chicken Stew and Dumplings

This down-home favourite has been given an uptown makeover. Caraway adds a hint of bistro chic, and the airy, tomato-flavoured dumplings have all the society matrons politely clapping with delight. It's a big city sensation!

Bone-in chicken thighs, skin removed	1 1/2 lbs.	680 g
Chicken drumsticks, skin removed (see Note 1)	1 1/2 lbs.	680 g
Salt, sprinkle		
Pepper, sprinkle		
Butter (or hard margarine)	1 tbsp.	15 mL
Chopped onion	2 cups	500 mL
Paprika	2 tsp.	10 mL
Garlic clove, minced (or 1/4 tsp., 1 mL, powder)	1	1
Caraway seed, crushed (see Note 2)	1/2 tsp.	2 mL
Chopped fresh marjoram (or 1/8 tsp., 0.5 mL, dried)	1/2 tsp.	2 mL
All-purpose flour	1 tbsp.	15 mL
Chicken bouillon powder	1 tbsp.	15 mL
Water	3 cups	750 mL
DUMPLINGS		
All-purpose flour	2 1/4 cups	550 mL
Green onions, sliced	2	2
Baking powder	4 tsp.	20 mL
Salt	1 tsp.	5 mL
Vegetable cocktail juice	1 1/4 cups	300 mL
Cooking oil	1/4 cup	60 mL

Sprinkle chicken thighs and drumsticks with salt and pepper. Put into greased 4 quart (4 L) casserole. Set aside.

Melt butter in large frying pan on medium. Add onion. Cook for 5 to 10 minutes, stirring often, until softened.

Add next 4 ingredients. Heat and stir for 1 to 2 minutes until fragrant.

Add flour and bouillon powder. Heat and stir for 1 minute. Slowly add water, stirring constantly, until boiling and slightly thickened.

(continued on next page)

Oven Ovations

Pour over chicken. Bake, covered, in 350°F (175°C) oven for about 1 1/2 hours until chicken is fully cooked and internal temperature reaches 170°F (77°C).

Dumplings: Measure first 4 ingredients into medium bowl. Stir. Make a well in centre.

Add vegetable juice and cooking oil to well. Stir until just moistened. Spoon mounds of batter, about 2 tbsp. (30 mL) each, in single layer on top of chicken mixture. Bake, covered, for 20 minutes. Bake, uncovered, for another 5 minutes until wooden pick inserted in centre of dumpling comes out clean. Serves 6.

1 serving: 575 Calories; 22.1 g Total Fat (9.6 g Mono, 5.5 g Poly, 4.8 g Sat); 150 mg Cholesterol; 47 g Carbohydrate; 3 g Fibre; 45 g Protein; 1324 mg Sodium

Note 1: When removing skin from drumsticks, grasp skin with a paper towel. This will give a good grip on the otherwise slippery skin.

Note 2: If you don't have a mortar and pestle, crush caraway seed on a cutting board using the flat side of a chef's knife.

Chili-Rubbed Chicken

Is a friend or a family member's love of spicy food rubbing off on you? Return the favour by giving chicken a rub down with this spicy mixture. Serve with a crisp, cool salad and a baked potato.

Brown sugar, packed	2 tbsp.	30 mL
Chili powder	2 tbsp.	30 mL
Paprika	2 tsp.	10 mL
Garlic powder	1 tsp.	5 mL
Cayenne pepper	1/2 tsp.	2 mL
Bone-in chicken thighs (5 – 6 oz., 140 – 170 g, each)	8	8
Worcestershire sauce	2 tbsp.	30 mL

Combine first 5 ingredients in small cup.

Brush chicken with Worcestershire sauce. Rub spice mixture on chicken. Place on greased wire rack set in foil-lined baking sheet with sides. Bake in 375°F (190°C) oven for about 45 minutes until chicken is crispy and internal temperature reaches 170°F (77°C). Makes 8 thighs.

1 thigh: 157 Calories; 7.3 g Total Fat (2.7 g Mono, 1.8 g Poly, 2.0 g Sat); 60 mg Cholesterol; 5 g Carbohydrate; 1 g Fibre; 17 g Protein; 123 mg Sodium

Pictured on page 54.

Oven Ovations

Nacho Chicken Squares

From an adult perspective, think of it as lazy tacos. Serve with salsa.

Large eggs, fork-beaten	2	2
Coarsely crushed nacho chips	1 cup	250 mL
Grated sharp Cheddar (or mozzarella) cheese	1 cup	250 mL
Can of tomato sauce	7 1/2 oz.	213 mL
Fine dry bread crumbs	1/2 cup	125 mL
Finely chopped onion	1/2 cup	125 mL
Finely chopped jalapeño pepper (see Tip, page 33)	1 tbsp.	15 mL
Ground cumin	1 tsp.	5 mL
Salt	1 tsp.	5 mL
Pepper	1/2 tsp.	2 mL
Lean ground chicken	2 lbs.	900 g
TOPPING		
Sour cream	1 cup	250 mL
Chopped fresh chives (or green onion)	1/3 cup	75 mL

Combine first 10 ingredients in large bowl.

Add chicken. Mix well. Spread evenly in greased 9 x 13 inch (22 x 33 cm) baking pan. Bake in 375°F (190°C) oven for about 40 minutes until lightly browned and internal temperature reaches 175°F (80°C). Cut into 8 squares.

Topping: Combine sour cream and chives in small bowl. Spoon over squares. Serves 8

1 serving: 460 Calories; 29.9 g Total Fat (3.9 g Mono, 0.9 g Poly, 7.6 g Sat); 82 mg Cholesterol; 17 g Carbohydrate; 2 g Fibre; 28 g Protein; 783 mg Sodium

1. Chicken Paella, page 82
2. Coconut Curry Casserole, page 60

Props courtesy of: Browne & Co.

Pesto-Stuffed Chicken

Play hide and seek with this spectacular chicken dish! Your guests will be delighted to discover a layer of creamy pesto hidden just beneath the skin of these tender chicken breasts. Decadent and delicious!

Herb and garlic cream cheese	6 tbsp.	100 mL
Finely diced red pepper	1/4 cup	60 mL
Basil pesto	2 tbsp.	30 mL
Salt	1/4 tsp.	1 mL
Pepper	1/4 tsp.	1 mL
Bone-in chicken breast halves (10 – 11 oz., 285 – 310 g, each)	4	4

Combine first 5 ingredients in small bowl.

Carefully loosen chicken skin but do not remove (see Note). Stuff cream cheese mixture between meat and skin, spreading mixture as evenly as possible. Secure skin with wooden picks. Place chicken, skin-side up, on greased baking sheet with sides. Bake in 350°F (175°C) oven for about 50 minutes until fully cooked and internal temperature reaches 170°F (77°C). Remove wooden picks. Serves 4.

1 serving: 298 Calories; 11.4 g Total Fat (0.6 g Mono, 0.5 g Poly, 1.6 g Sat); 132 mg Cholesterol; 1 g Carbohydrate; trace Fibre; 44 g Protein; 434 mg Sodium

Note: To loosen chicken skin, lift edge of skin and gently slide fingers as far as possible underneath skin. Be careful not to tear the skin.

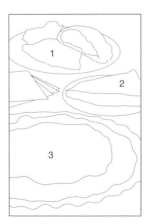

1. Picadillo Pastries, page 64
2. Pizza-Style Meatloaf, page 84
3. Honey Garlic Crostata, page 75

Props courtesy of: Winners Stores

Italian Burgers

Spezia, or spice, is what makes these Italian-inspired patties extra nice!
Adjust the amount of chilies to suit your preferred heat level. Very flavourful!

Large egg, fork-beaten	1	1
Fresh bread crumbs (see Note 1)	3/4 cup	175 mL
Dijon mustard	2 tsp.	10 mL
Garlic clove, minced (or 1/2 tsp., 1 mL, powder)	1	1
Fennel seed, crushed (see Note 2)	1/2 tsp.	2 mL
Dried crushed chilies	1/2 tsp.	2 mL
Dried oregano	1/2 tsp.	2 mL
Salt	1/2 tsp.	2 mL
Pepper	1/2 tsp.	2 mL
Lean ground chicken	1 lb.	454 g
Sun-dried tomato pesto	2 1/2 tbsp.	37 mL
Sliced roasted red peppers, blotted dry	1 cup	250 mL
Slices of mozzarella cheese	8	8
Lettuce leaves	8	8
Tomato slices	8	8
Hamburger buns, split	8	8

Combine first 9 ingredients in large bowl.

Add chicken. Mix well. Divide into 8 equal portions. Shape into 3 inch (7.5 cm) diameter patties.

Arrange patties on greased baking sheet with sides. Broil on top rack in oven for about 5 minutes until top is lightly browned. Turn. Spread pesto on patties. Broil for another 5 minutes until browned.

Arrange red pepper on patties. Place cheese slices over red pepper. Broil for about 2 minutes until cheese is melted.

Serve patties, topped with lettuce and tomato, in buns. Makes 8 burgers.

1 burger: 380 Calories; 19.0 g Total Fat (3.7 g Mono, 1.5 g Poly, 5.3 g Sat); 50 mg Cholesterol; 28 g Carbohydrate; 2 g Fibre; 23 g Protein; 677 mg Sodium

Pictured on page 53.

Note 1: To make fresh bread crumbs, tear bread slices into smaller pieces and process in blender until they form crumbs.

Note 2: If you don't have a mortar and pestle, crush fennel seed on a cutting board using the flat side of a chef's knife.

Honey Garlic Crostata

Sweet and saucy chicken and vegetables crowned with golden puff pastry.

Liquid honey	1/4 cup	60 mL
Dry sherry	2 tbsp.	30 mL
Soy sauce	2 tbsp.	30 mL
Garlic cloves, minced	4	4
Dijon mustard	1 tbsp.	15 mL
Pepper	1/2 tsp.	2 mL
Sesame oil (optional)	1 tsp.	5 mL
Cooking oil	2 tsp.	10 mL
Boneless, skinless chicken breast halves, cut into 1 inch (2.5 cm) cubes	1/2 lb.	225 g
Cooking oil	2 tsp.	10 mL
Chopped onion	1 cup	250 mL
Chopped red pepper	1 cup	250 mL
Frozen mixed vegetables	1 cup	250 mL
Package of puff pastry (14 oz., 397 g), thawed according to package directions	1/2	1/2

Combine first 7 ingredients in small bowl. Set aside.

Heat first amount of cooking oil in large frying pan on medium-high. Add chicken. Cook for 2 to 3 minutes, stirring occasionally, until browned. Remove to plate. Reduce heat to medium.

Add second amount of cooking oil to same frying pan. Add onion and red pepper. Cook for 5 to 10 minutes, stirring often, until onion is golden. Add chicken and honey mixture. Stir. Cook for 3 minutes. Add frozen vegetables. Stir. Transfer to large bowl. Cool.

Roll out puff pastry on lightly floured surface to 11 inch (28 cm) diameter circle. Place on baking sheet. Spoon chicken mixture onto centre of pastry, leaving 2 inch (5 cm) edge. Fold a section of edge up and over edge of filling. Repeat with next section, allowing pastry to overlap so that a fold is created. Repeat until pastry border is completely folded around filling. Bake in 375°F (190°C) oven for 25 to 30 minutes until pastry is puffed and golden. Let stand for 5 minutes before serving. Serves 4.

1 serving: 640 Calories; 32.2 g Total Fat (17.4 g Mono, 4.0 g Poly, 7.9 g Sat); 33 mg Cholesterol; 62 g Carbohydrate; 4 g Fibre; 22 g Protein; 1272 mg Sodium

Pictured on page 72.

Spinach Chicken Lasagna

Where's the beef? Chicken lasagna's where it's at. With lots of sauce, rich flavours and a tempting appearance, this dish is sure to best its beef brother.

Water	16 cups	4 L
Salt	2 tsp.	10 mL
Spinach lasagna noodles	12	12
Cooking oil	1 1/2 tbsp.	25 mL
Boneless, skinless chicken breast halves, chopped	1 3/4 lbs.	790 g
Sliced fresh white mushrooms	2 cups	500 mL
Chopped onion	1 1/2 cups	375 mL
Chopped red pepper	1 1/2 cups	375 mL
Garlic cloves, minced (or 1/2 tsp., 2 mL, powder)	2	2
Tomato pasta sauce	4 cups	1 L
Chopped fresh spinach leaves, lightly packed	2 cups	500 mL
Can of diced tomatoes (with juice)	14 oz.	398 mL
Dried oregano	2 tsp.	10 mL
Dried basil	1 tsp.	5 mL
Salt	1/4 tsp.	1 mL
Pepper	1/8 tsp.	0.5 mL
Cayenne pepper (optional)	1/4 tsp.	1 mL
2% cottage cheese	1 1/2 cups	375 mL
Crumbled feta cheese	1/2 cup	125 mL
Grated Parmesan cheese	1/3 cup	75 mL
Dried thyme	1/2 tsp.	2 mL
Pepper	1/2 tsp.	2 mL
Dried rosemary, crushed	1/4 tsp.	1 mL
Grated mozzarella and Cheddar cheese blend	2 cups	500 mL
Parsley flakes	2 tsp.	10 mL

(continued on next page)

Combine water and salt in Dutch oven or large pot. Bring to a boil. Add noodles. Boil, uncovered, for 12 to 14 minutes, stirring occasionally, until tender but firm. Drain. Rinse with cold water. Drain well. Set aside.

Heat cooking oil in same pot on medium-high. Add chicken. Cook for 8 to 10 minutes, stirring occasionally, until no longer pink. Remove to plate. Reduce heat to medium.

Add next 4 ingredients to same pot. Cook for about 10 minutes, stirring often, until onion is softened.

Add next 8 ingredients and chicken. Stir. Simmer, covered, for 10 minutes, stirring occasionally, to blend flavours. Remove from heat. Set aside.

Combine next 6 ingredients in medium bowl.

To assemble, layer ingredients in greased 9 x 13 inch (22 x 33 cm) baking pan as follows:

1. 1 cup (250 mL) chicken mixture
2. 3 lasagna noodles
3. 3 cups (750 mL) chicken mixture
4. 3 lasagna noodles
5. Cottage cheese mixture
6. 3 lasagna noodles
7. 3 cups (750 mL) chicken mixture
8. 3 lasagna noodles
9. Remaining chicken mixture

Combine cheese blend and parsley in medium bowl. Sprinkle over top. Cover with greased foil. Bake in 350°F (175°F) oven for 60 minutes. Remove foil. Bake for another 30 minutes until cheese is bubbling and starting to turn golden. Let stand for 10 minutes before serving. Serves 8.

1 serving: 574 Calories; 22.8 g Total Fat (5.2 g Mono, 1.6 g Poly, 9.8 g Sat); 99 mg Cholesterol; 46.9 g Carbohydrate; 11 g Fibre; 48 g Protein; 1325 mg Sodium

Pictured on page 89.

Paré Pointer

Talk about zones. We have the Arctic zone,
the Temperate zone and the Tow-Away zone.

Chicken Shepherd's Pie

Although shepherds usually mind their sheep, this rebel shepherd minds a flock of chickens! Join the rebellion and enjoy this take on a classic favourite.

Water, approximately	3 cups	750 mL
Peeled potatoes, cut into 2 inch (5 cm) pieces (about 3 medium)	1 1/2 lbs.	680 g
Large egg, fork-beaten	1	1
Grated sharp Cheddar cheese	2/3 cup	150 mL
Milk	2 tbsp.	30 mL
Salt	1/2 tsp.	2 mL
Pepper	1/4 tsp.	1 mL
Cooking oil	1 tbsp.	15 mL
Lean ground chicken	1 1/2 lbs.	680 g
Garlic clove, minced (or 1/4 tsp., 1 mL, powder)	1	1
Chopped onion	2 cups	500 mL
Frozen peas and carrots	4 cups	1 L
Can of condensed cream of chicken soup	10 oz.	284 mL
Dried sage	1 tsp.	5 mL
Salt	1/4 tsp.	1 mL
Pepper	1/2 tsp.	2 mL

Pour about 1 inch (2.5 cm) of water into large saucepan. Add potato. Cover. Bring to a boil. Reduce heat to medium. Boil gently for 12 to 15 minutes until tender. Drain. Return to same pot.

Add next 5 ingredients. Mash. Cover to keep warm.

Heat cooking oil in large frying pan on medium. Add chicken and garlic. Scramble-fry for 5 minutes. Add onion. Cook for about 5 minutes, stirring occasionally, until onion is softened and chicken is no longer pink.

Add remaining 5 ingredients. Heat and stir for about 5 minutes until boiling. Transfer to greased 3 quart (3 L) shallow baking dish. Spoon potato mixture over top. Spread evenly. Using fork, score decorative pattern on potato mixture. Bake, uncovered, in 350°F (175°C) oven for 30 to 40 minutes until bubbling and golden. Serves 6.

1 serving: 521 Calories; 26.1 g Total Fat (2.9 g Mono, 1.2 g Poly, 4.1 g Sat); 48 mg Cholesterol; 43 g Carbohydrate; 6 g Fibre; 31 g Protein; 824 mg Sodium

Cordon Bleu Bake

We've made this blue-ribbon favourite fuss-free. No fiddly prep is required to achieve this fine French flavour. Serve with steamed veggies and bon appétit!

Water	10 cups	2.5 L
Salt	1 1/4 tsp.	6 mL
Medium egg noodles	6 cups	1.5 L
Cooking oil	1 tbsp.	15 mL
Boneless, skinless chicken breast halves, cut into 1/2 inch (12 mm) strips	1 1/2 lbs.	680 g
Butter (or hard margarine)	2 tbsp.	30 mL
Fine dry bread crumbs	1/2 cup	125 mL
Butter (or hard margarine)	3 tbsp.	50 mL
All-purpose flour	1/4 cup	60 mL
Milk	3 3/4 cups	925 mL
Grated Gruyère (or Swiss) cheese	2 cups	500 mL
Deli (or Black Forest) ham, chopped	6 oz.	170 mL

Combine water and salt in Dutch oven or large pot. Bring to a boil. Add noodles. Boil, uncovered, for about 4 minutes, stirring occasionally, until tender but firm. Drain. Return to same pot. Cover to keep warm.

Heat cooking oil in large frying pan on medium. Add chicken. Cook for about 10 minutes, stirring occasionally, until browned. Remove to plate.

Melt first amount of butter in medium saucepan on medium. Add bread crumbs. Stir well. Transfer to small bowl. Wipe saucepan clean.

Melt second amount of butter in same saucepan on medium. Add flour. Heat and stir for 1 minute.

Slowly add milk, stirring constantly with whisk, until smooth. Heat and stir for about 5 minutes until boiling and thickened. Remove from heat.

Add cheese. Stir until smooth. Add to noodles.

Add chicken and ham. Stir until coated. Spread evenly in 9 x 13 inch (22 x 33 cm) baking dish. Sprinkle bread crumb mixture over top. Bake in 375°F (190°C) oven for about 25 minutes until bubbling and edges are starting to brown. Let stand for 10 minutes before serving. Serves 6.

1 serving: 701 Calories; 29.5 g Total Fat (8.5 g Mono, 2.8 g Poly, 15.1 g Sat); 197 mg Cholesterol; 52 g Carbohydrate; 2 g Fibre; 55 g Protein; 800 mg Sodium

Sunday Fried Chicken

For those who prefer to wade rather than sink when they're frying, we've "shallow fried" then baked this crispy chicken delight just for you. Start marinating on Saturday for dinner on Sunday—and don't forget a side of coleslaw.

Bone-in chicken thighs (5 – 6 oz., 140 – 170 g, each)	6	6
Chicken drumsticks (3 – 5 oz., 85 – 140 g, each)	6	6
Buttermilk	1 1/2 cups	375 mL
Water	1 1/2 cups	375 mL
Louisiana hot sauce	1 tbsp.	15 mL
Soy sauce	1 tbsp.	15 mL
Worcestershire sauce	1 tsp.	5 mL
Garlic powder	1/2 tsp.	2 mL
All-purpose flour	1 cup	250 mL
Onion powder	1 tsp.	5 mL
Salt	1 tsp.	5 mL
Pepper	1/2 tsp.	2 mL
Baking powder	1/2 tsp.	2 mL
Cayenne pepper	1/2 tsp.	2 mL
Poultry seasoning	1/2 tsp.	2 mL
Seasoned salt	1 tsp.	5 mL
Cooking oil, approximately	3 cups	750 mL

Put chicken into large resealable freezer bag.

Combine next 6 ingredients in small bowl. Pour over chicken. Seal bag. Turn until coated. Let stand in refrigerator for 12 to 24 hours, turning occasionally. Remove chicken. Do not pat dry. Discard any remaining buttermilk mixture.

Combine next 7 ingredients in separate large resealable freezer bag. Add chicken in batches. Toss until coated. Discard any remaining flour mixture. Place chicken on baking sheet. Let stand for 10 minutes.

Sprinkle chicken with seasoned salt.

(continued on next page)

Heat 1/2 inch (12 mm) cooking oil in large frying pan or large pot on medium-high until hot. Add half of chicken pieces. Cook for about 3 minutes per side until golden. Transfer to wire rack set in baking sheet with sides. Repeat with remaining chicken. Bake chicken in 375°F (190°C) oven for 20 to 30 minutes until fully cooked and internal temperature reaches 170°F (77°C). Serves 6.

1 serving: 336 Calories; 15.7 g Total Fat (7.2 g Mono, 4.1 g Poly, 3.0 g Sat); 98 mg Cholesterol; 17 g Carbohydrate; 1 g Fibre; 29 g Protein; 836 mg Sodium

Pictured on page 53.

Mushroom Swiss Strata

A smart Swiss miss will tell you that grated Swiss cheese will give a chicken casserole an unexpected flavour twist.

Cooking oil	1 tbsp.	15 mL
Lean ground chicken	1 lb.	454 g
Sliced fresh white mushrooms	4 cups	1 L
Chopped onion	1 cup	250 mL
Diced whole wheat (or white) bread	6 cups	1.5 L
Large eggs	6	6
Milk	2 cups	500 mL
Dijon mustard	1 tbsp.	15 mL
Parsley flakes	1 tbsp.	15 mL
Salt	1/4 tsp.	1 mL
Pepper	1/4 tsp.	1 mL
Grated Swiss cheese	2 cups	500 mL

Heat cooking oil in large frying pan on medium-high. Add chicken. Scramble-fry for 5 minutes. Add mushrooms and onion. Cook for about 10 minutes, stirring often, until onion is softened and mushrooms are lightly browned.

Place 2 cups (500 mL) diced bread in greased 3 quart (3 L) round casserole. Spread 1 cup (250 mL) chicken mixture over top. Repeat layers with remaining bread and chicken mixture.

Whisk next 6 ingredients in medium bowl until smooth. Pour over top.

Sprinkle with cheese. Press down lightly. Bake, uncovered, in 350°F (175°C) oven for about 50 minutes until puffed and golden. Let stand for 10 minutes before serving. Cut into wedges. Serves 8.

1 serving: 389 Calories; 22.4 g Total Fat (5.2 g Mono, 1.7 g Poly, 6.7 g Sat); 167 mg Cholesterol; 20 g Carbohydrate; 2 g Fibre; 28 g Protein; 402 mg Sodium

Chicken Paella

*They exclaim in Spain that paella (pi-AY-yuh) should often be
your main (course). We've used saffron, though it's a tad
pricey, to give this dish an authentic taste and look.*

Cooking oil	1 tsp.	5 mL
Boneless, skinless chicken thighs	8	8
(about 3 oz., 85 g, each)		
Chicken (or turkey) sausages, halved	6	6
(about 6 1/2 oz., 184 g)		
Chopped onion	1 cup	250 mL
Sliced red pepper	3/4 cup	175 mL
Sliced green pepper	1/2 cup	125 mL
Jalapeño pepper, finely diced	1	1
(see Tip, page 33)		
Garlic clove, minced (or 1/4 tsp.,	1	1
1 mL, powder)		
Can of diced tomatoes (with juice)	14 oz.	398 mL
Dry (or alcohol-free) white wine	1/2 cup	125 mL
Dried thyme	1 tsp.	5 mL
Paprika	1/2 tsp.	2 mL
Long grain white rice	1 1/4 cups	300 mL
Saffron threads (or turmeric)	1/8 tsp.	0.5 mL
Prepared chicken broth	1 1/2 cups	375 mL
Frozen peas	2 cups	500 mL
Can of artichoke hearts,	14 oz.	398 mL
drained and quartered		
Frozen, uncooked large shrimp	1/2 lb.	225 g
(peeled and deveined), thawed		

Heat cooking oil in large frying pan on medium. Add chicken. Cook for
3 to 4 minutes per side until browned. Transfer to 4 quart (4 L) casserole.

Add sausage to same frying pan. Cook for 5 to 10 minutes, turning
occasionally, until browned on all sides. Transfer to casserole. Arrange
chicken and sausage evenly in bottom of casserole.

Drain and discard all but 2 tsp. (10 mL) drippings from frying pan.

(continued on next page)

Oven Ovations

Add next 5 ingredients. Cook for about 5 minutes, stirring occasionally, until vegetables are tender-crisp.

Add next 4 ingredients. Bring to a boil. Reduce heat to medium. Cook for about 5 minutes, stirring occasionally and scraping any brown bits from bottom of pan, until thickened.

Add rice and saffron. Stir until rice is coated. Add broth. Bring to a boil. Remove from heat. Spoon rice mixture around chicken and sausage in casserole. Bake, covered, in 375°F (190°C) oven for 45 minutes.

Scatter remaining 3 ingredients over rice mixture. Bake, covered, for another 15 minutes until artichokes and peas are heated through and shrimp are pink and curled. Serves 8.

1 serving: 398 Calories; 11.5 g Total Fat (4.1 g Mono, 2.5 g Poly, 3.8 g Sat); 116 mg Cholesterol, 39 g Carbohydrate; 5 g Fibre; 33 g Protein; 480 mg Sodium

Pictured on page 71 and back cover.

Cajun Chicken Strips

Don't feel the least bit cagey about serving these baked bites for an entree or appetizer. Serve with ranch or blue cheese salad dressing as a cooling dip.

Cornflake crumbs	3/4 cup	175 mL
Paprika	1 tbsp.	15 mL
Dried basil	2 tsp.	10 mL
Dried oregano	2 tsp.	10 mL
Garlic powder	1 tsp.	5 mL
Seasoned salt	1 tsp.	5 mL
Cayenne pepper	1 tsp.	5 mL
Large eggs	2	2
Chicken breast cutlets, cut lengthwise into 12 strips	1 lb.	454 g
Cooking spray		

Combine first 7 ingredients in small shallow bowl.

Beat eggs with a fork in separate small shallow bowl.

Dip 1 chicken strip into egg. Press both sides into crumb mixture until evenly coated. Place on greased baking sheet with sides. Repeat with remaining chicken, egg and crumb mixture. Discard any remaining egg and crumb mixture. Spray strips with cooking spray. Bake in 425°F (220°C) oven for 15 to 20 minutes until no longer pink inside. Makes 12 strips.

1 strip: 71 Calories; 1.5 g Total Fat (0.5 g Mono, 0.3 g Poly, 0.4 g Sat); 45 mg Cholesterol; 4 g Carbohydrate; trace Fibre; 10 g Protein; 146 mg Sodium

Pizza-Style Meatloaf

Turn your dining experience upside down and inside out with this unique meatloaf that looks like a pizza! Instead of a traditional crust, the toppings sit over a thin, round meatloaf!

Cooking oil	2 tsp.	10 mL
Lean ground chicken	1 1/2 lbs.	680 g
Large eggs, fork-beaten	2	2
Grated havarti cheese	1/2 cup	125 mL
Fine dry bread crumbs	1/4 cup	60 mL
Lemon pepper	1 tsp.	5 mL
Dried tarragon	1/2 tsp.	2 mL
Tomato sauce	1/3 cup	75 mL
Basil pesto	2 tbsp.	30 mL
Grated havarti cheese	2/3 cup	150 mL
Thinly sliced red onion	1/2 cup	125 mL
Thinly sliced red pepper	1 cup	250 mL
Thinly sliced green pepper	1 cup	250 mL
Grated jalapeño Monterey Jack cheese	2/3 cup	150 mL

Heat cooking oil in large frying pan on medium-high. Add chicken. Scramble-fry for 5 to 10 minutes until no longer pink. Drain. Transfer to large bowl. Cool.

Add next 5 ingredients. Stir well. Press chicken mixture into bottom and halfway up sides of greased 12 inch (30 cm) deep dish pizza pan. Bake in 400°F (205°C) oven for about 5 minutes until firm and cheese is melted. Let stand for 5 minutes.

Combine tomato sauce and pesto in small cup. Spread evenly over chicken mixture.

Sprinkle second amount of havarti cheese over top. Layer next 3 ingredients, in order given, over cheese.

Sprinkle with Monterey Jack cheese. Bake for another for 15 to 20 minutes until cheese is melted and golden. Cut into wedges. Serves 6.

1 serving: 467 Calories; 31.4 g Total Fat (2.8 g Mono, 0.9 g Poly, 8.7 g Sat); 93 mg Cholesterol; 8 g Carbohydrate; 1 g Fibre; 35 g Protein; 459 mg Sodium

Pictured on page 72.

Chicken Cobbler

*Cobbler isn't just for dessert anymore! This savoury chicken version
is topped with golden biscuits. Make it a gobbler cobbler
by using chopped cooked turkey instead of chicken.*

Cooking oil	2 tsp.	10 mL
Thinly sliced fresh white mushrooms	2 cups	500 mL
Chopped onion	1 cup	250 mL
Diced green pepper	1/2 cup	125 mL
All-purpose flour	2 tbsp.	30 mL
Prepared chicken broth	1 1/4 cups	300 mL
Tomato paste (see Tip, page 105)	2 tbsp.	30 mL
Dried thyme	1/2 tsp.	2 mL
Pepper	1/2 tsp.	2 mL
Chopped cooked chicken (see Tip, page 26)	2 1/2 cups	625 mL
Frozen cut green beans	1 cup	250 mL
Sour cream	1/4 cup	60 mL
Worcestershire sauce	2 tsp.	10 mL
Biscuit mix	1 1/2 cups	375 mL
Grated medium Cheddar cheese	1/3 cup	75 mL
Milk	1/3 cup	75 mL
Grated medium Cheddar cheese	1/2 cup	125 mL

Heat cooking oil in large frying pan on medium. Add next 3 ingredients.
Cook for 5 to 10 minutes, stirring often, until onion is softened.

Add flour. Heat and stir for 1 minute.

Slowly add broth, stirring constantly, until smooth. Heat and stir until
boiling and thickened. Add next 3 ingredients. Stir. Remove from heat.

Add next 4 ingredients. Stir gently. Transfer to 2 quart (2 L) shallow
baking dish.

Combine biscuit mix and first amount of cheese in medium bowl.
Add milk. Stir until soft dough forms. Turn out onto lightly floured surface.
Shape into a ball. Pat dough to fit dimensions of baking dish. Place over
chicken mixture.

Sprinkle with second amount of cheese. Bake, uncovered, in 400°F (205°C)
oven for about 20 minutes until heated through and top is golden. Serves 4.

*1 serving: 551 Calories; 24.4 g Total Fat (6.0 g Mono, 2.4 g Poly, 9.9 g Sat); 101 mg Cholesterol;
44 g Carbohydrate; 3 g Fibre; 37 g Protein; 1149 mg Sodium*

Fiesta Torta

A fiesta of chicken, beans, cheese and salsa sandwiched between layers of tortilla.

Cooking oil	2 tsp.	10 mL
Lean ground chicken	1 lb.	454 g
Chopped onion	1/2 cup	125 mL
Lime juice	1 tbsp.	15 mL
Ground cumin	1 tsp.	5 mL
Garlic clove, minced (or 1/4 tsp., 1 mL, powder)	1	1
Can of red kidney beans, rinsed and drained	19 oz.	540 mL
Salsa	1 cup	250 mL
Roasted red peppers, drained and blotted dry, cut into strips	1/2 cup	125 mL
Can of diced green chilies	4 oz.	113 g
Chili powder	1 tsp.	5 mL
Flour tortillas (9 inch, 22 cm, diameter)	5	5
Grated Mexican cheese blend	3 cups	750 mL

Heat cooking oil in large frying pan on medium-high. Add chicken. Scramble-fry for about 5 minutes until no longer pink.

Add next 4 ingredients. Cook for about 5 minutes, stirring often, until onion is softened. Set aside.

Mash beans in medium bowl. Add next 4 ingredients. Stir.

To assemble, layer ingredients in greased 3 quart (3 L) round casserole as follows:

1. 1 tortilla (fold edge if necessary to fit casserole)
2. 1/2 of chicken mixture
3. 3/4 cup (175 mL) cheese
4. 1 tortilla
5. 1/2 of bean mixture
6. 1 tortilla
7. Remaining chicken mixture
8. 3/4 cup (175 mL) cheese
9. 1 tortilla
10. Remaining bean mixture
11. 1 tortilla
12. Remaining cheese

(continued on next page)

Oven Ovations

Bake, covered, in 375°F (190°C) oven for 45 minutes. Bake, uncovered, for another 20 minutes until cheese is golden. Let stand for 15 minutes before serving. Cut into wedges. Serves 8.

1 serving: 550 Calories; 26.3 g Total Fat (2.5 g Mono, 1.1 g Poly, 10.0 g Sat); 38 mg Cholesterol; 47 g Carbohydrate; 8 g Fibre; 28 g Protein; 982 mg Sodium

----

Tarragon Butter Chicken

Butter up the guests at your next dinner party with this juicy roast chicken. The herb butter is applied underneath the skin for extra flavour and moistness.

Butter (or hard margarine), softened	1/4 cup	60 mL
Dijon mustard (with whole seeds)	2 tbsp.	30 mL
Finely chopped green onion	2 tbsp.	30 mL
Chopped fresh tarragon (or 3/4 tsp., 4 mL, dried)	1 tbsp.	15 mL
Garlic clove, minced (or 1/4 tsp., 1 mL, powder)	1	1
Whole chicken	3 – 3 1/2 lbs.	1.4 – 1.6 kg
Cooking oil	1 tbsp.	15 mL
Salt	1 tsp.	5 mL
Pepper	1/2 tsp.	2 mL
Prepared chicken broth	1 1/2 cups	375 mL

Combine first 5 ingredients in small bowl.

Carefully loosen chicken skin but do not remove (see Note). Stuff butter mixture between meat and skin, spreading mixture as evenly as possible.

Rub cooking oil over surface of chicken. Sprinkle with salt and pepper. Tie wings with butcher's string close to body. Tie legs to tail. Place on greased wire rack set in small roasting pan.

Bake, uncovered, in 350°F (175°C) oven for 1 1/2 to 2 hours, basting with broth every 30 minutes, until meat thermometer inserted in thickest part of breast reads 180°F (83°C). Remove chicken from oven. Cover with foil. Let stand for 10 minutes before carving. Serves 4.

1 serving: 641 Calories; 49.7 g Total Fat (19.2 g Mono, 8.8 g Poly, 17.3 g Sat); 198 mg Cholesterol; 2 g Carbohydrate; trace Fibre; 44 g Protein; 1268 mg Sodium

Note: To loosen chicken skin, lift edge of skin and gently slide fingers as far as possible underneath skin. Be careful not to tear the skin.

Zippy Anise Drumsticks

Anise, anise, we've got a crush on you! For those of you who haven't experimented with aniseed yet, join the love train and give the subtle licorice flavour a go.

Brown sugar, packed	3 tbsp.	50 mL
Aniseed, crushed (see Note)	1 tbsp.	15 mL
Dried crushed chilies	3/4 tsp.	4 mL
Salt	1/2 tsp.	2 mL
Chicken drumsticks (3 – 5 oz., 85 – 140 g, each)	12	12
Olive oil	3 tbsp.	50 mL

Combine first 4 ingredients in small cup.

Brush chicken with olive oil. Rub aniseed mixture over chicken. Place on greased wire rack set in foil-lined baking sheet with sides. Bake in 400°F (205°C) oven for about 40 minutes, turning at halftime, until fully cooked and internal temperature reaches 170°F (77°C). Makes 12 drumsticks.

1 drumstick: 153 Calories; 7.8 g Total Fat (3.9 g Mono, 1.4 g Poly, 1.6 g Sat); 65 mg Cholesterol; 4 g Carbohydrate; trace Fibre; 16 g Protein; 174 mg Sodium

Note: If you don't have a mortar and pestle, crush aniseed on a cutting board using the flat side of a chef's knife.

1. Spinach Chicken Lasagna, page 76

Props courtesy of: Casa Bugatti

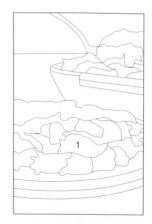

Rosemary Tomato Sauce

Subtle spices make this dish a simple delight. Serve on pasta.

All-purpose flour	2 tbsp.	30 mL
Boneless, skinless chicken thighs, halved	1 lb.	454 g
Chopped tomato	2 1/4 cups	550 mL
Chopped onion	1 cup	250 mL
Chopped yellow pepper	1 cup	250 mL
Dry (or alcohol-free) white wine	1 cup	250 mL
Tomato paste (see Tip, page 105)	1/3 cup	75 mL
Finely chopped fresh rosemary, (or 3/4 tsp., 4 mL, dried, crushed)	1 tbsp.	15 mL
Garlic cloves, minced (or 1/2 tsp., 2 mL, powder)	2	2
Bay leaf	1	1
Granulated sugar	1 tsp.	5 mL
Salt	1/4 tsp.	1 mL
Pepper	1/2 tsp.	2 mL

Measure flour into large resealable freezer bag. Add chicken. Seal bag. Toss until coated. Transfer chicken to 3 1/2 to 4 quart (3.5 to 4 L) slow cooker. Discard any remaining flour

Combine remaining 11 ingredients in large bowl. Pour over chicken. Cook, covered, on Low for 8 to 10 hours or on High for 4 to 5 hours. Discard bay leaf. Makes about 5 cups (1.25 L).

1 cup (250 mL): 240 Calories; 7.3 g Total Fat (2.7 g Mono, 1.8 g Poly, 2.0 g Sat); 59 mg Cholesterol; 17 g Carbohydrate; 3 g Fibre; 19 g Protein; 201 mg Sodium

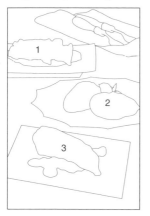

1. Uptown Asparagus Chicken, page 58
2. Lemon Basil Chicken Rolls, page 62
3. Festive Chicken Bake, page 65

Props courtesy of: Casa Bugatti
Cherison Enterprises Inc.
Danesco Inc.
Pier 1 Imports
Stokes

Chicken And Lentils

Consider the Zen nature of stew—all the ingredients working together to infuse one with warmth and peace. Now that's something to meditate on!

All-purpose flour	2 tbsp.	30 mL
Salt	1/2 tsp.	2 mL
Pepper	1/2 tsp.	2 mL
Bone-in chicken thighs, skin removed (5 – 6 oz., 140 – 170 g, each)	8	8
Cooking oil	1 tbsp.	15 mL
Chopped carrot	1 cup	250 mL
Chopped onion	1 cup	250 mL
Sliced peeled tart apple (such as Granny Smith)	2 cups	500 mL
Apple juice	1 cup	250 mL
Dried green lentils	1/2 cup	125 mL
Dry (or alcohol-free) red wine	1/2 cup	125 mL
Raisins	1/2 cup	125 mL
Grated orange zest	1 tsp.	5 mL
Ground cinnamon	1/2 tsp.	2 mL
Bay leaf	1	1
Chopped fresh parsley	3 tbsp.	50 mL
Salt	1/4 tsp.	1 mL

Combine first 3 ingredients in large resealable freezer bag. Add chicken. Seal bag. Toss until coated. Remove chicken. Discard any remaining flour mixture.

Heat cooking oil in large frying pan on medium. Add chicken. Cook for about 10 minutes, turning occasionally, until browned on all sides. Transfer with slotted spoon to plate. Set aside.

Add carrot and onion to same frying pan. Cook for 5 to 10 minutes, stirring often, until onion is softened. Transfer to 3 1/2 to 4 quart (3.5 to 4 L) slow cooker. Arrange chicken over top.

Combine next 8 ingredients in large bowl. Pour over chicken. Cook, covered, on Low for 8 to 10 hours or on High for 4 to 5 hours. Discard bay leaf.

Add parsley and salt. Stir gently. Serves 4.

1 serving: 693 Calories; 20.9 g Total Fat (8.3 g Mono, 4.9 g Poly, 4.9 g Sat); 143 mg Cholesterol; 76 g Carbohydrate; 7 g Fibre; 46 g Protein; 504 mg Sodium

Tangy Pineapple Chicken

Let your taste buds be fickle tonight. Sweet? Sour?
Let them have it all—in one delightfully tangy dish!

Chopped onion	1 cup	250 mL
Sliced carrots	1 cup	250 mL
Sliced celery	1 cup	250 mL
Finely grated gingerroot (or 1/2 tsp., 2 mL, ground ginger)	2 tsp.	10 mL
All-purpose flour	1/4 cup	60 mL
Curry powder	2 tsp.	10 mL
Salt	1/2 tsp.	2 mL
Pepper	1/4 tsp.	1 mL
Boneless, skinless chicken thighs (about 3 oz., 85 g, each)	8	8
Can of diced tomatoes (with juice)	14 oz.	398 mL
Can of pineapple tidbits (with juice)	14 oz.	398 mL
Ketchup	1/4 cup	60 mL

Put first 4 ingredients into 4 quart (4 L) slow cooker.

Combine next 4 ingredients in large resealable freezer bag. Add chicken. Seal bag. Toss until coated. Arrange chicken over vegetables. Sprinkle with any remaining flour mixture.

Combine remaining 3 ingredients in medium bowl. Pour over chicken. Cook, covered, on Low for 5 to 6 hours or on High for 2 1/2 to 3 hours. Stir. Serves 4.

1 serving: 392 Calories; 13.2 g Total Fat (5.0 g Mono, 3.1 g Poly, 3.6 g Sat); 112 mg Cholesterol; 35 g Carbohydrate; 3 g Fibre; 33 g Protein; 899 mg Sodium

Pictured on page 107.

Paré Pointer
The big difference between the North Pole and
the South Pole is the whole world.

In A Pickle Stew

This cheeky combination will both astound and amuse your guests—delightful!

Red baby potatoes, larger ones cut in half	1 lb.	454 g
Bacon slices, diced	3	3
All-purpose flour	2 tbsp.	30 mL
Salt	1/2 tsp	2 mL
Pepper	1/2 tsp.	2 mL
Boneless, skinless chicken thighs, cut into 1 1/2 inch (3.8 cm) pieces	1 1/2 lbs.	680 g
Chopped onion	2 cups	500 mL
Chopped fresh white mushrooms	1 1/2 cups	375 mL
Paprika	2 tsp.	10 mL
Dry (or alcohol-free) white wine	1/2 cup	125 mL
Chicken bouillon cubes (1/5 oz., 6 g, each), crumbled	2	2
Water	1 cup	250 mL
Water	1/4 cup	60 mL
All-purpose flour	1 tbsp.	15 mL
Diced dill pickle	1/2 cup	125 mL

Chopped fresh dill, for garnish

Put potatoes into 3 1/2 to 4 quart (3.5 to 4 L) slow cooker.

Cook bacon in large frying pan on medium for about 3 minutes, stirring occasionally, until crisp. Transfer with slotted spoon to paper towel-lined plate to drain. Set aside. Reserve drippings in pan.

Combine next 3 ingredients in large resealable freezer bag. Add chicken. Seal bag. Toss until coated. Remove chicken. Discard any remaining flour mixture. Heat reserved drippings in same frying pan on medium. Add chicken. Cook for about 8 minutes, turning occasionally, until browned. Transfer with slotted spoon to slow cooker.

Add onion and mushrooms to same frying pan. Cook for about 5 to 10 minutes, stirring often, until onion is softened. Transfer to slow cooker.

Add next 4 ingredients to slow cooker. Stir. Cook, covered, on Low for 4 to 6 hours or High for 2 to 3 hours.

(continued on next page)

Stir second amount of water into second amount of flour in small cup until smooth. Add to slow cooker. Stir well. Cook, covered, on High for about 15 minutes until sauce is thickened. Add pickle and bacon. Stir.

Garnish with dill. Makes about 8 cups (2 L).

1 cup (250 mL): 254 Calories; 10.4 g Total Fat (5.2 g Mono, 2.3 g Poly, 4.0 g Sat); 62 mg Cholesterol; 18 g Carbohydrate; 2 g Fibre; 19 g Protein; 674 mg Sodium

Lemon Chicken Bean Stew

The favourite combination of chicken and lemon has never "bean" so tasty. Bright citrus picks up this simple and satisfying stew. Serve with baby potatoes or a salad.

All-purpose flour	1/4 cup	60 mL
Boneless, skinless chicken thighs, halved	2 lbs.	900 g
Chopped carrot	2 cups	500 mL
Can of white kidney beans, rinsed and drained	19 oz.	540 mL
Prepared chicken broth	1 cup	250 mL
Apple juice	1/2 cup	125 mL
Salt	1/2 tsp.	2 mL
Pepper	1/4 tsp.	1 mL
Chopped fresh parsley (or 2 1/4 tsp., 11 mL, flakes)	3 tbsp.	50 mL
Lemon juice	1 tbsp.	15 mL
Grated lemon zest	1 tsp.	5 mL

Measure flour into large resealable freezer bag. Add chicken. Seal bag. Toss until coated. Remove chicken. Discard any remaining flour.

Put carrot into 3 1/2 to 4 quart (3.5 to 4 L) slow cooker. Arrange chicken over top. Scatter beans over chicken.

Combine next 4 ingredients in small bowl. Pour over beans. Cook, covered, on Low for 8 to 9 hours or on High for 4 to 4 1/2 hours.

Add remaining 3 ingredients. Stir. Makes about 5 cups (1.25 L).

1 cup (250 mL): 438 Calories; 15.0 g Total Fat (5.3 g Mono, 3.3 g Poly, 3.9 g Sat); 119 mg Cholesterol; 35 g Carbohydrate; 6 g Fibre; 40 g Protein; 575 mg Sodium

Mushroom Chicken Sauce

This delicious sauce cooks while you're out and about. Put some pasta on when you get home and dinner's on the table in minutes!

Bacon slices, diced	6	6
Cooking oil	1 tbsp.	15 mL
Chopped onion	1 cup	250 mL
Sliced fresh white mushrooms	3 cups	750 mL
Paprika	1 tsp.	5 mL
Garlic cloves, minced (or 1/2 tsp., 2 mL, powder)	2	2
All-purpose flour	3 tbsp.	50 mL
Salt	1/4 tsp.	1 mL
Pepper	1/4 tsp.	1 mL
Boneless, skinless chicken thighs, cut into 3/4 inch (2 cm) cubes	1 1/2 lbs.	680 g
Dry (or alcohol-free) white wine	1/2 cup	125 mL
Prepared chicken broth	1/2 cup	125 mL
Frozen peas	1/2 cup	125 mL
Chopped fresh parsley (or 1 tbsp., 15 mL, flakes)	1/4 cup	60 mL
Sour cream	1/4 cup	60 mL

Cook bacon in large frying pan on medium for about 5 minutes, stirring occasionally, until almost crisp. Transfer with slotted spoon to paper towels to drain. Drain and discard drippings from pan.

Heat cooking oil in same frying pan on medium. Add onion. Cook for 5 to 10 minutes, stirring often, until softened.

Add next 3 ingredients. Cook for about 5 minutes, stirring occasionally, until mushrooms are softened. Add bacon. Stir. Spread evenly in 3 1/2 to 4 quart (3.5 to 4 L) slow cooker.

Combine next 3 ingredients in large resealable freezer bag. Add chicken. Seal bag. Toss until coated. Arrange chicken over mushroom mixture. Discard any remaining flour mixture.

Pour wine and broth over chicken. Cook, covered, on Low for 8 to 9 hours or on High for 4 to 4 1/2 hours.

(continued on next page)

Add remaining 3 ingredients. Stir. Cook, covered, on High for about 10 minutes until heated through. Makes about 5 1/4 cups (1.3 L).

1 cup (250 mL): 344 Calories; 17.7 g Total Fat (6.7 g Mono, 3.5 g Poly, 5.3 g Sat); 100 mg Cholesterol; 11 g Carbohydrate; 2 g Fibre; 30 g Protein; 413 mg Sodium

Pictured on page 107.

Curious Chicken Chili

Curious as to why this chili is such a curiosity? Check out the ingredients. You just have to taste this delightful concoction—we know you want to.

Cooking oil	2 tsp.	10 mL
Boneless, skinless chicken thighs, cut into 1/2 inch (12 mm) pieces	1 lb.	454 g
Chopped onions	1 1/2 cups	375 mL
Chopped green pepper	1 cup	250 mL
Diced jalapeño pepper (see Tip, page 33)	1 tbsp.	15 mL
Garlic cloves, minced (or 1/2 tsp., 2 mL, powder)	2	2
Salt	1 tsp.	5 mL
Can of diced tomatoes (with juice)	14 oz.	398 mL
Can of pineapple chunks (with juice)	14 oz.	398 ml
Can of red kidney beans, rinsed and drained	14 oz.	398 mL
Hot (or cold) strong prepared coffee	1 cup	250 mL
Can of diced green chilies	4 oz.	113 g
Tomato paste (see Tip, page 105)	3 tbsp.	50 mL
Chili powder	2 tbsp.	30 mL
Semi-sweet chocolate baking square (1 oz., 28 g), grated	1	1
Ground cumin	1 tsp.	5 mL

Heat cooking oil in large frying pan on medium-high. Add chicken. Cook for about 5 minutes, stirring often, until browned.

Add next 5 ingredients. Cook for about 5 minutes, stirring often, until onion starts to soften. Transfer to 3 1/2 to 4 quart (3.5 to 4 L) slow cooker.

Add remaining 9 ingredients. Stir. Cook, covered, on Low for 4 hours or on High for 2 hours. Makes about 8 cups (2 L).

1 cup (250 mL): 246 Calories; 7.2 g Total Fat (2.4 g Mono, 1.5 g Poly, 2.0 g Sat); 37 mg Cholesterol; 31 g Carbohydrate; 7 g Fibre; 16 g Protein; 505 mg Sodium

Chicken Fricassee

Any fine French chef will tell you that fricassee is meat stewed in a white cream sauce. But never worry that this dish will pale by comparison— the carrot, red pepper and peas add nice shots of colour.

Chopped carrot	2 cups	500 mL
Chopped celery	1 1/2 cups	375 mL
Chopped red pepper	1 1/2 cups	375 mL
Boneless, skinless chicken breast halves, halved	1 lb.	454 g
Boneless, skinless chicken thighs	1 lb.	454 g
Sliced leek (white part only)	3 1/2 cups	875 mL
Butter (or hard margarine)	3 tbsp.	50 mL
Garlic cloves, minced (or 1/2 tsp., 2 mL, powder), optional	2	2
All-purpose flour	1/4 cup	60 mL
Prepared chicken broth	2 cups	500 mL
Dry (or alcohol-free) white wine	1/4 cup	60 mL
Can of artichoke hearts, drained and halved	14 oz.	398 mL
Dried thyme	1 tsp.	5 mL
Seasoned salt	1 tsp.	5 mL
Pepper	1/4 tsp.	1 mL
Frozen peas	2 cups	500 mL
Can of evaporated milk	5 1/2 oz.	160 mL

Layer first 6 ingredients, in order given, in 4 to 5 quart (4 to 5 L) slow cooker.

Melt butter in medium saucepan on medium. Add garlic. Heat and stir for about 1 minute until fragrant. Add flour. Heat and stir for 1 minute.

Slowly add broth and wine, stirring constantly, until smooth. Heat and stir for about 7 minutes until boiling and thickened. Remove from heat.

Add next 4 ingredients. Stir. Pour over chicken mixture in slow cooker. Cook, covered, on Low for 8 to 9 hours or on High for 4 to 4 1/2 hours.

Add peas and evaporated milk. Stir. Cook, covered, on High for about 15 minutes until peas are tender. Serves 8.

1 serving: 342 Calories; 11.9 g Total Fat (3.6 g Mono, 1.7 g Poly, 5.3 g Sat); 87 mg Cholesterol; 27 g Carbohydrate; 7 g Fibre; 31 g Protein; 622 mg Sodium

Cranberry Chicken

Take it slow with this cranberry-sauced chicken. Just let the flavours spend the
day mingling in your slow cooker and you'll have a dinner that's worth the wait.

Chopped carrot	3/4 cup	175 mL
Chopped onion	3/4 cup	175 mL
Can of whole cranberry sauce	14 oz.	398 mL
Hickory barbecue sauce	1/2 cup	125 mL
Ketchup	1/2 cup	125 mL
Brown sugar, packed	1/3 cup	75 mL
Dijon mustard	2 tbsp.	30 mL
Lemon juice	1 tbsp.	15 mL
Dried crushed chilies	1/2 tsp.	2 mL
Chicken legs, back attached (11 – 12 oz., 310 – 340 g, each), skin removed	6	6
Dried sage	1 tsp.	5 mL
Garlic powder	1/2 tsp.	2 mL
Pepper	1/2 tsp.	2 mL

Chopped fresh parsley, for garnish

Put carrot and onion into 4 to 5 quart (4 to 5 L) slow cooker.

Combine next 7 ingredients in medium bowl.

Sprinkle both sides of chicken with next 3 ingredients. Arrange 3 chicken
legs over vegetables. Spoon half of cranberry mixture over chicken. Repeat
with remaining chicken and cranberry mixture. Cook, covered, on Low for
6 to 7 hours or on High for 3 to 3 1/2 hours. Transfer chicken with slotted
spoon to serving dish. Spoon vegetables around chicken. Skim and discard
fat from sauce. Serve sauce on the side.

Garnish chicken and vegetables with parsley. Serves 6.

1 serving: 620 Calories; 15.4 g Total Fat (4.7 g Mono, 3.8 g Poly, 3.9 g Sat); 250 mg Cholesterol;
57 g Carbohydrate; 2 g Fibre; 63 g Protein; 844 mg Sodium

Pictured on page 107.

Chicken Rice Casserole

Get the classic flavour of a cheesy Parmesan and garlic risotto—without all that stirring! Your nearest and dearest will never suspect that your slow cooker did all the work.

Long grain brown rice	1 1/2 cups	375 mL
Chopped onion	1 cup	250 mL
Chopped red pepper	1 cup	250 mL
Sliced carrot (1/4 inch, 6 mm, thick slices)	1 cup	250 mL
Fresh (or frozen) whole green beans	4 cups	1 L
All-purpose flour	1/4 cup	60 mL
Grated Parmesan cheese	1/4 cup	60 mL
Paprika	1 1/2 tsp.	7 mL
Garlic powder	1/2 tsp.	2 mL
Pepper	1/2 tsp.	2 mL
Boneless, skinless chicken breast halves, halved	1 lb.	454 g
Boneless, skinless chicken thighs	1 lb.	454 g
Cooking oil	1 tbsp.	15 mL
Prepared chicken broth	1 1/2 cups	375 mL
Can of condensed cream of mushroom soup	10 oz.	284 mL
Dry (or alcohol-free) white wine	1/3 cup	75 mL

Combine first 4 ingredients in greased 5 to 7 quart (5 to 7 L) slow cooker.

Layer green beans over rice mixture.

Combine next 5 ingredients in large resealable freezer bag. Add chicken. Seal bag. Toss until coated. Remove chicken. Reserve any remaining flour mixture.

Heat cooking oil in large frying pan on medium. Add chicken. Cook for 2 to 3 minutes per side until browned. Arrange chicken over green beans. Sprinkle with reserved flour mixture.

Combine remaining 3 ingredients in same frying pan. Cook on medium for about 5 minutes, stirring occasionally and scraping any brown bits from bottom of pan, until smooth. Pour over chicken. Cook, covered, on Low for 7 to 8 hours or on High for 3 1/2 to 4 hours. Serves 8.

1 serving: 400 Calories; 11.5 g Total Fat (4.0 g Mono, 2.8 g Poly, 3.0 g Sat); 73 mg Cholesterol; 41 g Carbohydrate; 5 g Fibre; 31 g Protein; 519 mg Sodium

Raspberry Chicken

*Rah, rah raspberry! Three cheers for this MVI (most valuable ingredient).
Sweet yet tangy, all the stats agree—this dish is a sure winner!*

Raspberry jam	1/2 cup	125 mL
Dry (or alcohol-free) white wine	1/3 cup	75 mL
Raspberry red wine vinegar	1/4 cup	60 mL
Soy sauce	1 tbsp.	15 mL
Dijon mustard	1 tsp.	5 mL
Garlic clove, minced (or 1/4 tsp., 1 mL, powder)	1	1
Chicken legs, back attached (11 – 12 oz., 310 – 340 g, each), skin removed	4	4
Water	2 tbsp.	30 mL
Cornstarch	1 tbsp.	15 mL

Chopped fresh parsley, for garnish

Combine first 6 ingredients in small bowl. Transfer to large resealable freezer bag. Add chicken. Seal bag. Turn until coated. Let stand in refrigerator for at least 4 hours or overnight, turning occasionally. Transfer chicken with raspberry mixture to 1 1/2 to 2 quart (1.5 to 2 L) slow cooker. Cook, covered, on Low for 6 to 8 hours or High for 3 to 4 hours. Remove chicken to serving dish with slotted spoon or tongs. Cover to keep warm. Skim fat from sauce.

Stir water into cornstarch in small cup. Add to slow cooker. Stir. Cook, covered, on High for about 5 minutes until boiling and thickened. Pour over chicken.

Garnish with parsley. Serves 4.

1 serving: 525 Calories; 15 g Total Fat (4.7 g Mono, 3.8 g Poly, 3.9 g Sat); 250 mg Cholesterol; 29 g Carbohydrate; trace Fibre; 62 g Protein; 607 mg Sodium

Paré Pointer

*She was into clothing. For dinner she served
jacket potatoes and button mushrooms.*

Ginger Pineapple Meatballs

Talk about a well-balanced meal! These tangy meatballs are not too sweet, not too sour, and not too spicy. Serve this saucy delight over jasmine rice.

Large egg, fork-beaten	1	1
Fine dry bread crumbs	1/2 cup	125 mL
Finely chopped red pepper	1/4 cup	60 mL
Grated onion	1/4 cup	60 mL
Ground ginger	1/2 tsp.	2 mL
Salt	1/2 tsp.	2 mL
Pepper	1/4 tsp.	1 mL
Lean ground chicken	1 lb.	454 g
Cooking oil	2 tsp.	10 mL
Can of crushed pineapple (with juice)	14 oz.	398 mL
Sweet chili sauce	1/2 cup	125 mL
Lime juice	1 tbsp.	15 mL
Finely grated gingerroot (or 1/2 tsp., 2 mL, ground ginger)	2 tsp.	10 mL
Salt	1/4 tsp.	1 mL
Soy sauce	1 tbsp.	15 mL
Cornstarch	2 tsp.	10 mL
Sliced green onion	1/4 cup	60 mL

Combine first 7 ingredients in medium bowl.

Add chicken. Mix well. Roll into 1 inch (2.5 cm) balls.

Heat cooking oil in large frying pan on medium-high. Add meatballs. Cook for 5 to 10 minutes, turning often, until fully cooked and internal temperature reaches 175°F (80°C). Transfer with slotted spoon to paper towel-lined plate to drain. Makes about 40 meatballs.

Add next 5 ingredients to same frying pan. Stir soy sauce into cornstarch in small cup. Add to pineapple mixture. Heat and stir until boiling and thickened. Add meatballs. Stir until coated. Reduce heat to medium-low. Cook for about 5 minutes until heated through.

Sprinkle with green onion. Serves 4.

1 serving: 423 Calories; 19.7 g Total Fat (2.2 g Mono, 1.1 g Poly, 0.7 g Sat); 47 mg Cholesterol; 35 g Carbohydrate; 4 g Fibre; 24 g Protein; 1439 mg Sodium

Pictured on page 126.

Fragrant Chicken And Rice

Now, this is what we call aromatherapy! As this wholesome, zesty rice dish simmers, revel in the soothing and delicious fragrance that will silently beckon everyone to the kitchen!

Cooking oil	1 tbsp.	15 mL
Boneless, skinless chicken thighs, cut into 1 inch (2.5 cm) pieces	1 lb.	454 g
Chopped onion	2 cups	500 mL
Ground cinnamon	1/2 tsp.	2 mL
Ground coriander	1/2 tsp.	2 mL
Ground cumin	1/2 tsp.	2 mL
Garlic powder	1/4 tsp.	1 mL
Pepper	1/4 tsp.	1 mL
Prepared chicken broth	2 1/2 cups	625 mL
Can of chickpeas (garbanzo beans), rinsed and drained	19 oz.	540 mL
Long grain white rice	1 cup	250 mL
Chopped dried apricot	1/2 cup	125 mL
Salt	1/4 tsp.	1 mL
Sliced natural almonds, toasted (see Tip, page 13)	1/2 cup	125 mL
Chopped fresh chives	2 tbsp.	30 mL
Grated lemon zest	1/2 tsp.	2 mL

Heat cooking oil in large frying pan on medium. Add chicken. Cook for about 5 minutes, stirring occasionally, until starting to brown. Remove to plate.

Add onion to same frying pan. Cook for 5 to 10 minutes, stirring occasionally, until softened.

Add next 5 ingredients. Heat and stir for about 1 minute until fragrant.

Add next 5 ingredients and chicken. Stir. Bring to a boil. Reduce heat to medium-low. Simmer, covered, for 30 minutes, without stirring. Remove from heat. Let stand, covered, for about 5 minutes until liquid is absorbed and rice is tender. Fluff with fork.

Add remaining 3 ingredients. Toss gently. Makes about 8 cups (2 L).

1 cup (250 mL): 387 Calories; 11.4 g Total Fat (5.2 g Mono, 3.1 g Poly, 1.9 g Sat); 37 mg Cholesterol; 50 g Carbohydrate; 5.2 g Fibre; 21 g Protein; 508 mg Sodium

Chicken Cacciatore

Catch the scent of this savoury cacciatore and you'll be the one caught in its tantalizing spell. The herbed tomato sauce will have you ensnared. You won't be able to break free—but that's OK, you won't mind at all! Goes great over pasta or rice.

Cooking oil	2 tsp.	10 mL
Boneless, skinless chicken thighs, quartered	1 1/2 lbs.	680 g
Sliced fresh white mushrooms	1 1/2 cups	375 mL
Chopped onion	1 cup	250 mL
Garlic cloves, minced (or 1/2 tsp., 2 mL, powder)	2	2
Dry (or alcohol-free) white wine	1/4 cup	60 mL
Can of diced tomatoes (with juice)	28 oz.	796 mL
Chopped green pepper	1 1/2 cups	375 mL
Tomato paste (see Tip, page 105)	1/4 cup	60 mL
Bay leaf	1	1
Dried basil	1 tsp.	5 mL
Dried oregano	1 tsp.	5 mL
Granulated sugar	1 tsp.	5 mL
Dried rosemary, crushed	1/2 tsp.	2 mL
Salt	1/2 tsp.	2 mL
Pepper	1/4 tsp.	1 mL

Heat cooking oil in large saucepan or Dutch oven on medium-high. Add chicken. Cook, uncovered, for about 5 minutes, stirring occasionally, until chicken starts to brown.

Add next 3 ingredients. Cook for 5 to 10 minutes, stirring occasionally, until onion is softened and liquid from mushrooms has evaporated.

Add wine. Heat and stir for 1 minute.

Add remaining 10 ingredients. Stir. Bring to a boil. Reduce heat to medium-low. Cook, partially covered, for about 30 minutes, stirring occasionally, until chicken is no longer pink inside and green pepper is tender. Discard bay leaf. Makes about 8 cups (2 L).

1 cup (250 mL): 186 Calories; 7.7 g Total Fat (3.1 g Mono, 1.9 g Poly, 1.9 g Sat); 56 mg Cholesterol; 11 g Carbohydrate; 2 g Fibre; 17 g Protein; 481 mg Sodium

Creamy Spinach Meat Sauce

This velvety sauce is strong to the finish because it's made with spinach!
Great for serving on toast or in puff pastry shells. Use a bit more
milk to thin this sauce if you want to serve it over pasta.

Ingredient	Imperial	Metric
Olive (or cooking) oil	2 tsp.	10 mL
Lean ground chicken	1 lb.	454 g
Chopped onion	1/2 cup	125 mL
Garlic cloves, minced (or 1/2 tsp., 2 mL, powder)	2	2
Ground coriander	1/2 tsp.	2 mL
Ground cumin	1/2 tsp.	2 mL
Ground nutmeg	1/4 tsp.	1 mL
Salt	3/4 tsp.	4 mL
Pepper	1/8 tsp.	0.5 mL
All-purpose flour	2 tbsp.	30 mL
Can of evaporated milk	13 1/2 oz.	385 mL
Milk	1 cup	250 mL
Box of frozen chopped spinach, thawed and squeezed dry	10 oz.	300 g

Heat olive oil in large frying pan on medium-high. Add next 8 ingredients. Scramble-fry for about 8 minutes until chicken is no longer pink and onion is softened.

Sprinkle with flour. Heat and stir for 1 minute. Reduce heat to medium.

Slowly add evaporated milk, stirring constantly, until smooth. Add milk. Heat and stir for about 5 minutes until boiling and thickened.

Add spinach. Stir. Simmer, uncovered, for about 2 minutes, stirring occasionally, until heated through. Makes about 4 cups (1 L).

1 cup (250 mL): 443 Calories; 26.0 g Total Fat (4.1 g Mono, 0.5 g Poly, 5.3 g Sat); 31 mg Cholesterol; 22 g Carbohydrate; 2.8 g Fibre; 31 g Protein; 739 mg Sodium

 tip If a recipe calls for less than an entire can of tomato paste, freeze the unopened can for 30 minutes. Open both ends and push the contents through one end. Slice off only what you need. Freeze the remaining paste in a resealable freezer bag or plastic wrap for future use.

Ginger Chicken Stir-Fry

Ginger chicken with pea pods—so hot, it's cool!

Boneless, skinless chicken breast halves	1 lb.	454 g
Sesame (or cooking) oil	1 tbsp.	15 mL
Sugar snap peas, trimmed	2 cups	500 mL
Apple juice	1/2 cup	125 mL
Chopped green onion	1/3 cup	75 mL
Honey	2 tbsp.	30 mL
Soy sauce	2 tbsp.	30 mL
Finely grated gingerroot	2 tsp.	10 mL
Dried crushed chilies	1/2 tsp.	2 mL
Seasoned salt	1/2 tsp.	2 mL
Water	1/4 cup	60 mL
Cornstarch	1 1/2 tsp.	7 mL

Place 1 chicken breast between 2 sheets of plastic wrap. Pound with mallet or rolling pin to 1/4 inch (6 mm) thickness. Repeat with remaining chicken. Cut chicken crosswise into thin strips.

Heat wok or large frying pan on medium-high until very hot. Add sesame oil. Add chicken. Stir-fry for 4 to 5 minutes until no longer pink. Add next 8 ingredients. Stir. Cook for about 3 minutes, stirring often, until peas are tender-crisp.

Stir water into cornstarch in small cup. Add to chicken mixture. Heat and stir until boiling and thickened. Serves 4.

1 serving: 287 Calories; 5.4 g Total Fat (1.8 g Mono, 1.9 g Poly, 1.0 g Sat); 66 mg Cholesterol; 30 g Carbohydrate; 2 g Fibre; 28 g Protein; 912 mg Sodium

1. Tangy Pineapple Chicken, page 93
2. Mushroom Chicken Sauce, page 96
3. Cranberry Chicken, page 99

Props courtesy of: Emile Henry

Stovetop Stunners

Chicken Sloppy Joes

*If they were called Tidy Joes they just wouldn't be as much fun, would they?
Unleash your inner child and dive into these saucy open-faced sandwiches.*

Cooking oil	1 tbsp.	15 mL
Lean ground chicken	1 lb.	454 g
Chopped green pepper	1/2 cup	125 mL
Chopped onion	1/2 cup	125 mL
Tomato juice	1 cup	250 mL
Can of pizza sauce	7 1/2 oz.	213 mL
Ketchup	2 tbsp.	30 mL
Chili powder	1 tsp.	5 mL
Garlic powder	1/4 tsp.	1 mL
Salt	1/4 tsp.	1 mL
Hamburger buns, split and toasted	4	4

Heat cooking oil in large frying pan on medium-high. Add next 3 ingredients. Scramble-fry for 8 to 10 minutes until chicken is no longer pink.

Add next 6 ingredients. Stir. Reduce heat to medium-low. Simmer, covered, for 10 minutes to blend flavours.

Place bun halves on large plate. Spoon chicken mixture over bun halves. Makes 8 sloppy joes for 4 hungry people.

1 sloppy joe: 219 Calories; 10.8 g Total Fat (1.8 g Mono, 1.0 g Poly, 0.4 g Sat); 0 mg Cholesterol; 17 g Carbohydrate; 2 g Fibre; 13 g Protein; 454 mg Sodium

1. Fennel Roast Chicken, page 66

Props courtesy of: Cherison Enterprises Inc.

Cashew Chicken

If Asian flavour is what you're craving, don't bother with take-out.
Keep your cash in your pocket and your cashews in your wok.
Best served over rice.

Dry sherry	2 tbsp.	30 mL
Soy sauce	1 tbsp.	15 mL
Cornstarch	2 tsp.	10 mL
Chili paste (sambal oelek)	1 tsp.	5 mL
Finely grated gingerroot (or 1/4 tsp., 1 mL, ground ginger)	1 tsp.	5 mL
Garlic clove, minced (or 1/4 tsp., 1 mL, powder)	1	1
Sesame oil (optional)	2 tsp.	10 mL
Boneless, skinless chicken breast halves, cut into 1/2 inch (12 mm) pieces	1 1/2 lbs.	680 g
Prepared chicken broth	1/2 cup	125 mL
Cornstarch	1 tbsp.	15 mL
Hoisin sauce	1 tbsp.	15 mL
Soy sauce	1 tbsp.	15 mL
Chili paste (sambal oelek)	1 tsp.	5 mL
Dry sherry	1 tsp.	5 mL
Cooking oil	1 tbsp.	15 mL
Cooking oil	1 tbsp.	15 mL
Coarsely chopped onion	1 1/2 cups	375 mL
Small green pepper, cut into 3/4 inch (2 cm) pieces	1	1
Small red pepper, cut into 3/4 inch (2 cm) pieces	1	1
Can of bamboo shoots, drained	8 oz.	227 mL
Finely grated gingerroot (or 1/4 tsp., 1 mL, ground ginger)	1 1/2 tsp.	7 mL
Salted cashews	1 1/4 cups	300 mL
Chopped green onion	1/4 cup	60 mL

(continued on next page)

Whisk first 7 ingredients in a medium bowl.

Add chicken. Stir until coated. Let stand at room temperature for 15 minutes.

Stir next 6 ingredients in small bowl until smooth. Set aside.

Heat wok or large frying pan on medium-high until very hot. Add first amount of cooking oil. Add chicken mixture. Stir-fry for 2 to 3 minutes until chicken is no longer pink.

Add second amount of cooking oil to hot wok. Add next 5 ingredients. Stir-fry for 1 minute. Cook, covered, for 2 to 3 minutes, stirring occasionally, until peppers are tender-crisp. Stir broth mixture. Add to chicken mixture. Heat and stir for about 1 minute until boiling and thickened.

Add cashews and green onion. Stir. Serves 6.

1 serving: 554 Calories; 21.1 g Total Fat (6.0 g Mono, 6.6 g Poly, 4.9 g Sat); 245 mg Cholesterol; 29 g Carbohydrate; 8 g Fibre; 66 g Protein; 1387 mg Sodium

Pictured on page 126.

Paré Pointer

Johnny thought his dad should do his homework for him but his dad said it wouldn't be right. Johnny thought his dad could at least try.

Sweet Chicken Curry

Take your friends and family to India with an Asian-themed dinner.
Add basmati rice, naan bread and cucumber salad for a lively Indian meal.

Cooking oil	1 tbsp.	15 mL
Boneless, skinless chicken thighs, cut into 3/4 inch (2 cm) pieces	1 lb.	454 g
Chopped onion	1 cup	250 mL
Chopped celery	1/3 cup	75 mL
Curry powder	1 1/2 tsp.	7 mL
Ground ginger	1 tsp.	5 mL
Garlic clove, minced (or 1/4 tsp., 1 mL, powder)	1	1
Dried crushed chilies	1/2 tsp.	2 mL
Chopped peeled cooking apple (such as McIntosh)	1 cup	250 mL
Prepared chicken broth	1 cup	250 mL
Can of tomato sauce	7 1/2 oz.	213 mL
Golden raisins	1/4 cup	60 mL
Plain yogurt	1/2 cup	125 mL
Chopped fresh cilantro or parsley (or 1 1/2 tsp., 7 mL, dried)	2 tbsp.	30 mL
Chopped unsalted peanuts	1/4 cup	60 mL
Chopped fresh cilantro or parsley	2 tbsp.	30 mL

Heat cooking oil in large frying pan on medium-high. Add chicken. Cook for about 5 minutes, stirring occasionally, until browned.

Add next 6 ingredients. Cook for about 5 minutes, stirring often, until onion and celery start to soften.

Add next 4 ingredients. Stir. Bring to a boil. Reduce heat to medium-low. Simmer, uncovered, for about 15 minutes until thickened and apple is tender.

Add yogurt and first amount of cilantro. Cook and stir until heated through.

Sprinkle individual servings with peanuts and second amount of cilantro. Makes about 4 1/2 cups (1.1 L).

1 cup (250 mL): 321 Calories; 16.2 g Total Fat (7.1 g Mono, 4.1 g Poly, 3.6 g Sat); 70 mg Cholesterol; 22 g Carbohydrate; 3 g Fibre; 24 g Protein; 544 mg Sodium

Chicken Ratatouille

In need of a vacation? Send your taste buds on a trip with this robust dish that's full of bold Mediterranean flavours. This versatile dish (pronounced Ra-tuh-TOO-ee) goes great with crusty bread or pasta. Serve with lemon wedges.

All-purpose flour	1/4 cup	60 mL
Salt	1/2 tsp.	2 mL
Pepper	1/4 tsp.	1 mL
Boneless, skinless chicken thighs (about 3 oz., 85 g, each)	8	8
Cooking oil	1 tbsp.	15 mL
Diced eggplant (with peel)	2 cups	500 mL
Chopped onion	1 cup	250 mL
Can of diced tomatoes (with juice)	14 oz.	398 mL
Chopped green pepper	1 cup	250 mL
Sliced fresh white mushrooms	1 cup	250 mL
Granulated sugar	1 1/2 tsp.	7 mL
Dried basil	1 tsp.	5 mL
Drled thyme	1/2 tsp.	2 mL
Garlic powder	1/2 tsp.	2 mL
Salt	1/2 tsp.	2 mL

Combine first 3 ingredients in large resealable freezer bag. Add chicken. Toss until coated. Remove chicken. Discard any remaining flour mixture.

Heat cooking oil in large frying pan on medium-high. Add chicken. Cook for about 2 minutes per side until browned. Remove to plate.

Add eggplant and onion to same frying pan. Cook for about 5 minutes, stirring often and scraping any brown bits from bottom of pan, until browned and starting to soften.

Add remaining 8 ingredients and chicken. Stir. Bring to a boil. Reduce heat to medium-low. Simmer, covered, for about 30 minutes until chicken is no longer pink inside and vegetables are tender. Serves 4.

1 serving: 361 Calories; 16.5 g Total Fat (6.9 g Mono, 4.1 g Poly, 3.9 g Sat); 112 mg Cholesterol; 20 g Carbohydrate; 3 g Fibre; 34 g Protein; 879 mg Sodium

Pictured on page 125.

Sauerkraut Potato Stew

Say hello to Oktoberfest with this rollicking sauerkraut and beer stew.

Cooking oil	2 tsp.	10 mL
Sliced smoked ham sausage	3/4 lb.	340 g
All-purpose flour	1/4 cup	60 mL
Salt	1/2 tsp.	2 mL
Pepper	1/4 tsp.	1 mL
Bone-in chicken thighs, skin removed (5 – 6 oz., 140 – 170 g, each)	6	6
Chopped onion	1 1/2 cups	375 mL
Chopped carrot	1/2 cup	125 mL
Cubed peeled potato	3 cups	750 mL
Prepared chicken broth	1 1/2 cups	375 mL
Beer	1 cup	250 mL
Diced peeled cooking apple (such as McIntosh)	1 cup	250 mL
Apple juice	1/2 cup	125 mL
Bay leaf	1	1
Caraway seed	1/2 tsp.	2 mL
Jar of wine sauerkraut, drained	17 1/2 oz.	500 mL

Heat cooking oil in Dutch oven or large pot on medium. Add sausage. Cook, uncovered, for about 5 minutes, stirring occasionally, until lightly browned. Transfer with slotted spoon to medium bowl. Set aside.

Combine next 3 ingredients in large resealable freezer bag. Add chicken. Toss until coated. Remove chicken. Discard any remaining flour mixture. Add chicken to same pot. Cook on medium for about 5 minutes per side until browned. Add to sausage.

Add onion and carrot to same pot. Cook for 5 to 10 minutes, stirring often, until onion is softened.

Add next 7 ingredients and chicken mixture. Stir. Bring to a boil. Reduce heat to medium-low. Simmer, covered, for about 15 minutes until potato is tender.

Add sauerkraut. Stir. Cook, uncovered, for about 15 minutes until thickened. Discard bay leaf. Serves 6.

1 serving: 586 Calories; 28.5 g Total Fat (12.5 g Mono, 4.7 g Poly, 9.0 g Sat); 110 mg Cholesterol; 42 g Carbohydrate; 5 g Fibre; 37 g Protein; 1795 mg Sodium

Black Bean Chili

A fiesta in every bite! Serve this versatile recipe with warm, crusty rolls or tortilla chips, or on a bed of fresh greens for a quick and easy taco salad.

Cooking oil	2 tsp.	10 mL
Lean ground chicken	1 lb.	454 g
Chopped onion	1 1/2 cups	375 mL
Chopped celery	1/2 cup	125 mL
Chili powder	1 tbsp.	15 mL
Dried oregano	2 tsp.	10 mL
Garlic clove, minced (or 1/4 tsp., 1 mL, powder)	1	1
Can of stewed tomatoes	14 oz.	398 mL
Chopped red pepper	1 1/2 cups	375 mL
Frozen kernel corn	1 cup	250 mL
Can of tomato sauce	7 1/2 oz.	213 mL
Hot pepper sauce	1/2 tsp.	2 mL
Can of black beans, rinsed and drained	19 oz.	540 mL
Sliced green onion	1/4 cup	60 mL
Grated sharp Cheddar cheese	1/2 cup	125 mL
Chopped fresh cilantro or parsley (optional)	2 tbsp.	30 mL

Heat cooking oil in large frying pan on medium-high. Add chicken. Scramble-fry for about 5 minutes until no longer pink.

Add onion and celery. Cook for 5 to 10 minutes, stirring often, until onion is softened. Reduce heat to medium.

Add next 3 ingredients. Heat and stir for about 1 minute until fragrant.

Add next 5 ingredients. Stir. Bring to a boil. Reduce heat to medium-low. Simmer, covered, for 15 minutes to blend flavours.

Add beans and green onion. Stir. Cook for about 10 minutes until heated through.

Sprinkle with cheese and cilantro. Makes about 7 cups (1.75 L).

1 cup (250 mL): 345 Calories; 13.7 g Total Fat (1.7 g Mono, 0.9 g Poly, 2.0 g Sat); 8 mg Cholesterol; 35 g Carbohydrate; 8 g Fibre; 23 g Protein; 606 mg Sodium

Pictured on page 143.

Chicken And Olives

Do you know someone who's absolutely mad for olives?
Their favourite place on a Friday night is the deli's olive bar?
Well, make them this creamy tomato dish decked with olives and
you'll have a friend for life! Goes great over couscous or pasta.

Cooking oil	1 tbsp.	15 mL
Chicken drumsticks, skin removed (see Note)	12	12
3 – 5 oz. (85 – 140 g) each		
Chopped onion	2 cups	500 mL
Sliced fresh white mushrooms	1 1/2 cups	375 mL
Diced pepperoni	1 cup	250 mL
Can of Italian-style stewed tomatoes	19 oz.	540 mL
Can of condensed cream of mushroom soup	10 oz.	284 mL
Dry (or alcohol-free) white wine	1 cup	250 mL
Large pitted green olives, halved	1/3 cup	75 mL
Pitted whole black olives, halved	1/3 cup	75 mL
Bay leaf	1	1
Dried oregano	1/2 tsp.	2 mL
Chopped fresh parsley	1/4 cup	60 mL

Heat cooking oil in large frying pan on medium. Add chicken. Cook for about 15 minutes, turning occasionally, until browned. Remove to plate. Cover to keep warm.

Add next 3 ingredients to same frying pan. Cook for 5 to 10 minutes, stirring often, until onion is softened.

Add next 7 ingredients and chicken. Stir. Bring to a boil. Reduce heat to medium-low. Simmer, covered, for 15 to 20 minutes until internal temperature of chicken reaches 170°F (77°C). Discard bay leaf.

Sprinkle with parsley. Serves 6.

1 cup (250 mL): 485 Calories; 23.2 g Total Fat (10.1 g Mono, 4.2 g Poly, 6.3 g Sat); 150 mg Cholesterol; 18 g Carbohydrate; 2 g Fibre; 43 g Protein; 1315 mg Sodium

Pictured on page 125.

Note: When removing skin from drumsticks, grasp skin with a paper towel. This will give a good grip on the otherwise slippery skin.

Chunky Salsa Corn Stew

No need to serve cornbread on the side. This hearty chili is topped with cornmeal dumplings. It's a rustic delight the whole family will love.

Cooking oil	1 tbsp.	15 mL
Boneless, skinless chicken thighs, halved	1 lb.	454 g
Salt	1/2 tsp.	2 mL
Pepper	1/4 tsp.	1 mL
Chopped green pepper	2 cups	500 mL
Chopped onion	1 1/2 cups	375 mL
Chili powder	1 tbsp.	15 mL
Ground cumin	1 tsp.	5 mL
Red baby potatoes, halved	1 lb.	454 g
Can of diced tomatoes (with juice)	14 oz.	398 mL
Chunky salsa	1 1/2 cups	375 mL
Prepared chicken broth	1 1/2 cups	375 mL
Frozen kernel corn	1/2 cup	125 mL
Biscuit mix	1 1/3 cups	325 mL
Cornmeal	2/3 cup	150 mL
Milk	2/3 cup	150 mL
Frozen kernel corn, thawed	1/2 cup	125 mL
Chopped fresh cilantro or parsley (or 1 1/2 tsp., 7 mL, dried)	2 tbsp.	30 mL

Heat cooking oil in Dutch oven or large pot on medium. Add chicken. Sprinkle with salt and pepper. Cook, uncovered, for about 5 minutes, stirring occasionally, until starting to brown.

Add next 4 ingredients. Cook for 5 to 10 minutes, stirring occasionally, until vegetables are tender-crisp.

Add next 5 ingredients. Stir. Bring to a boil. Reduce heat to medium-low. Simmer, covered, for about 30 minutes until thickened and potato is tender.

Measure biscuit mix and cornmeal into medium bowl. Stir. Make a well in centre. Add remaining 3 ingredients to well. Stir until just moistened. Drop 2 tbsp. (30 mL) portions onto chicken mixture. Cook, covered, for about 20 minutes until wooden pick inserted into dumpling comes out clean. Serves 4.

1 serving: 710 Calories; 20.5 g Total Fat (9.4 g Mono, 4.4 g Poly, 4.9 g Sat); 77 mg Cholesterol; 96 g Carbohydrate; 10 g Fibre; 35 g Protein; 2134 mg Sodium

Chicken Cakes

Don't get all crabby about it! Believe us, you don't have to turn to crustaceans to make a delightful, little breaded cake. These chicken cakes are tender and just a little bit spicy.

SPICY DILL SAUCE

Mayonnaise	1/2 cup	125 mL
Dry sherry	1 tbsp.	15 mL
Chopped fresh dill (or 1/4 tsp., 1 mL, dried)	1 tsp.	5 mL
Cayenne pepper	1/4 tsp.	1 mL
Salt	1/4 tsp.	1 mL

CAKES

Boneless, skinless chicken breast halves (see Note 1)	1 lb.	454 g
Prepared chicken broth	1 1/2 cups	375 mL
Large egg, fork-beaten	1	1
Fine dry bread crumbs	1/3 cup	75 mL
Finely chopped onion	1/4 cup	60 mL
Finely chopped celery	2 tbsp.	30 mL
Finely chopped red pepper	2 tbsp.	30 mL
Chopped fresh dill (or 3/4 tsp., 4 mL, dried)	1 tbsp.	15 mL
Garlic clove, minced (or 1/4 tsp., 1 mL, powder)	1	1
Worcestershire sauce	1 tsp.	5 mL
Salt	1/2 tsp.	2 mL
Pepper	1/4 tsp.	1 mL
All-purpose flour	3 tbsp.	50 mL
Large eggs	2	2
Fine dry bread crumbs	1/3 cup	75 mL
Cooking oil	1 tbsp.	15 mL

Spicy Dill Sauce: Combine all 5 ingredients in small bowl. Makes about 1/2 cup (125 mL) sauce.

(continued on next page)

Stovetop Stunners

Cakes: Put chicken into small saucepan. Add broth. Bring to a boil. Reduce heat to medium-low. Simmer, covered, for about 10 minutes until no longer pink inside. Drain (see Note 2). Cool. Finely chop chicken. Set aside.

Combine next 10 ingredients in medium bowl. Add chicken and 3 tbsp. (50 mL) Spicy Dill Sauce. Stir gently until well combined. Divide into 8 equal portions. Shape into 1/2 inch (12 mm) thick cakes. Place cakes on waxed paper-lined baking sheet.

Measure flour onto plate.

Beat eggs in small shallow dish.

Measure bread crumbs onto separate plate. Press both sides of cakes into flour. Dip into egg. Press both sides of cakes into bread crumbs until coated. Discard any remaining flour, egg and bread crumbs.

Heat cooking oil in large frying pan on medium. Arrange cakes in single layer in frying pan. Cook for about 4 minutes per side until golden. Remove cakes to paper towel-lined plate to drain. Serve with remaining Spicy Dill Sauce. Makes 8 cakes.

1 cake with 2 tsp. (10 mL) sauce: 248 Calories; 15.8 g Total Fat (8.3 g Mono, 4.8 g Poly, 2.0 g Sat); 99 mg Cholesterol; 9 g Carbohydrate; trace Fibre; 17 g Protein; 454 mg Sodium

Note 1: If you have leftover cooked chicken, you can substitute 2 cups (500 mL) finely chopped cooked chicken for the chicken breast halves and omit the chicken broth.

Note 2: You can save the leftover chicken broth for another use. It makes an excellent broth for a bowl of chicken noodle soup!

Paré Pointer

The human cannonball at the circus needs a new job. He was fired.

Hoisin Chicken Pot

The sparkling flavours of hoisin and ginger make this dish a star attraction.

Chinese dried mushrooms	4	4
Boiling water	1 cup	250 mL
Cooking oil	1 tbsp.	15 mL
Bone-in chicken thighs, skin removed (5 – 6 oz., 140 – 170 g, each)	8	8
Chopped fresh white mushrooms	1 cup	250 mL
Medium onions, cut into 8 wedges each	2	2
Garlic cloves, minced	2	2
Finely grated gingerroot	2 tsp.	10 mL
Prepared chicken broth	2 cups	500 mL
Can of sliced water chestnuts, drained	8 oz.	227 mL
Hoisin sauce	1/2 cup	125 mL
Star anise	3	3
Chopped bok choy	8 cups	2 L
Chili paste (sambal oelek)	2 tsp.	10 mL
Finely chopped green onion	2 tbsp.	30 mL
Sesame seeds, toasted (see Tip, page 13)	1 tbsp.	15 mL

Put dried mushrooms into small heatproof bowl. Add boiling water. Stir. Let stand for about 20 minutes until softened. Drain. Remove and discard stems. Chop caps. Set aside.

Heat cooking oil in large saucepan or Dutch oven on medium-high. Add chicken. Cook, uncovered, for 3 to 4 minutes per side until browned. Remove to plate. Reduce heat to medium.

Add fresh mushrooms. Cook for about 3 minutes, stirring occasionally, until browned. Add next 3 ingredients. Cook for about 5 minutes, stirring occasionally, until onion starts to soften.

Add next 4 ingredients, dried mushrooms and chicken. Stir. Bring to a boil. Reduce heat to medium-low. Simmer, partially covered, for about 30 minutes until chicken is tender.

Add bok choy and chili paste. Stir. Cook for about 10 minutes, stirring occasionally, until bok choy is tender. Discard anise. Sprinkle with green onion and sesame seeds. Serves 4.

(continued on next page)

1 serving: *536 Calories; 23.2 g Total Fat (9.3 g Mono, 6.1 g Poly, 5.4 g Sat); 144 mg Cholesterol; 35 g Carbohydrate; 5 g Fibre; 47 g Protein; 1131 mg Sodium*

Pictured on page 126.

Mushroom Rice Skillet

Oven, stove, barbecue and microwave all going at the same time? Forget about it! Avoid a potential blackout and make your entire dinner using just your stovetop and a large frying pan. Rice, chicken, vegetables and minimal cleanup. How much easier can it get?

Cooking oil	1 tsp.	5 mL
Sliced fresh white mushrooms	2 cups	500 mL
Cooking oil	2 tsp.	10 mL
Boneless, skinless chicken thighs, cut into 1/2 inch (12 mm) strips	1 lb.	454 g
Chopped onion	2 cups	500 mL
Chopped tomato	2 cups	500 mL
Prepared chicken broth	2 cups	500 mL
Can of condensed cream of mushroom soup	10 oz.	284 mL
Long grain brown rice	1/2 cup	125 mL
Wild rice	1/2 cup	125 mL
Parsley flakes	1 tsp.	5 mL
Dried thyme	1/4 tsp.	1 mL
Pepper	1/4 tsp.	1 mL

Heat first amount of cooking oil in large frying pan on medium. Add mushrooms. Cook for about 10 minutes, stirring occasionally, until starting to brown. Remove to small bowl.

Add second amount of cooking oil to same frying pan. Add chicken. Cook for 5 to 10 minutes, stirring occasionally, until browned. Transfer with slotted spoon to plate.

Add onion to same frying pan. Cook for 5 to 10 minutes, stirring often, until softened.

Add remaining 8 ingredients, mushrooms and chicken. Stir. Bring to a boil. Reduce heat to medium-low. Simmer, covered, for about 1 hour, stirring occasionally, until rice is tender. Makes about 6 1/2 cups (1.6 L).

1 cup (250 mL): *306 Calories; 11.2 g Total Fat (4.1 g Mono, 2.9 g Poly, 2.5 g Sat); 46 mg Cholesterol; 33 g Carbohydrate; 3 g Fibre; 19 g Protein; 570 mg Sodium*

Lemon Asparagus Tortellini

Lemon can make even the creamiest dishes taste light and fresh. Delicious!

Water	12 cups	3 L
Salt	1 1/2 tsp.	7 mL
Fresh cheese-filled tortellini	12 1/2 oz.	350 g
Butter (or hard margarine)	2 tbsp.	30 mL
Finely chopped onion	1 cup	250 mL
Boneless, skinless chicken breast, cut into 3/4 inch (2 cm) cubes	1/2 lb.	225 g
Garlic cloves, minced	2	2
Salt	1/2 tsp.	2 mL
Pepper	1/4 tsp.	1 mL
Dry (or alcohol-free) white wine	2/3 cup	150 mL
Grated lemon zest	2 tsp.	10 mL
Fresh asparagus, trimmed of tough ends and cut into 2 inch (5 cm) pieces	1 lb.	454 g
Whipping cream	1 1/2 cups	375 mL
Finely chopped green onion	1 tbsp.	15 mL
Chopped fresh dill (or 1/2 tsp., 2 mL, dried)	1 1/2 tsp.	7 mL
Grated Parmesan cheese	2 tbsp.	30 mL
Finely chopped green onion	1 tbsp.	15 mL
Chopped fresh dill (or 1/2 tsp., 2 mL, dried)	1 1/2 tsp.	7 mL
Pepper, sprinkle		

Combine water and salt in Dutch oven or large pot. Bring to a boil. Add tortellini. Boil, uncovered, for about 8 minutes, stirring occasionally, until tender but firm. Drain. Set aside.

Melt butter in large frying pan on medium. Add next 5 ingredients. Cook for 5 to 10 minutes, stirring often, until onion starts to turn golden and chicken is no longer pink.

Add wine and lemon zest. Stir. Cook for about 5 minutes, stirring occasionally, until wine is reduced by half.

Add asparagus and whipping cream. Stir. Bring to a boil. Reduce heat to medium-low. Simmer, uncovered, for about 3 minutes until asparagus is tender-crisp.

(continued on next page)

Add first amounts of green onion and dill. Stir. Add tortellini. Cook and stir for about 2 minutes until heated through.

Sprinkle remaining 4 ingredients over top. Serve immediately. Makes about 7 cups (1.75 L).

1 cup (250 mL): 439 Calories; 25.9 g Total Fat (7.4 g Mono, 1.2 g Poly, 15.5 g Sat); 115 mg Cholesterol; 31 g Carbohydrate; 2 g Fibre; 18 g Protein;435 mg Sodium

---

Ginger Pear Chicken

"Pear" in mind that this tender, moist chicken has just a little heat from ginger.

Salt	1/2 tsp.	2 mL
Pepper	1/4 tsp.	1 mL
Ground ginger	1/4 tsp.	1 mL
Boneless, skinless chicken breast halves (4 – 6 oz., 113 – 170 g, each)	4	4
Olive (or cooking) oil	1 tbsp.	15 mL
Chopped onion	1/2 cup	125 mL
Finely grated gingerroot	1 tbsp.	15 mL
Diced peeled pear	2 cups	500 mL
Apple (or pear) cider	1 cup	250 mL
Balsamic vinegar	2 tbsp.	30 ml
Brown sugar, packed	1 tbsp.	15 mL
Chopped fresh thyme (or 1/4 tsp., 1 mL, dried)	1 tsp.	5 mL

Stir first 3 ingredients together in small cup. Sprinkle over chicken. Heat olive oil in large frying pan on medium-high. Add chicken. Cook for about 4 minutes, turning at halftime, until browned on both sides. Reduce heat to medium. Cook for another 6 to 8 minutes until chicken is fully cooked and internal temperature reaches 170°F (77°C). Remove to plate. Cover to keep warm.

Add onion and ginger to same frying pan. Cook for 2 to 3 minutes, stirring often, until onion starts to brown.

Add pear. Cook for 1 to 2 minutes, stirring occasionally, until pear starts to soften.

Add remaining 4 ingredients. Stir. Bring to a boil. Reduce heat to medium. Boil gently, uncovered, for about 10 minutes until pear issoftened and liquid is reduced by half. Add chicken. Cook, covered, for about 5 minutes until heated through. Serves 4.

1 serving: 263 Calories; 5.4 g Total Fat (3.0 g Mono, 0.7 g Poly, 1.0 g Sat); 66 mg Cholesterol; 27 g Carbohydrate; 3 g Fibre; 26 g Protein; 367 mg Sodium

Pineapple Chicken Bliss

Find your bliss in this saucy pineapple and coconut treat that has just enough
heat to keep you reaching for the water glass. Serve over a bed of hot jasmine rice.

Cooking oil	1 tsp.	5 mL
Boneless, skinless chicken breast halves, cut into 2 inch (5 cm) pieces	1 1/2 lbs.	680 g
Can of coconut milk	14 oz.	398 mL
Can of crushed pineapple, drained	14 oz.	398 mL
Chili sauce	1/2 cup	125 mL
Finely diced Thai hot chili pepper, (see Tip, page 33), or 1/8 tsp., 0.5 mL, cayenne pepper	1/4 tsp.	1 mL
Salt	1/4 tsp.	1 mL
Chopped fresh cilantro or parsley	3 tbsp.	50 mL

Heat cooking oil in large frying pan on medium-high. Add chicken. Cook for about 5 minutes, stirring occasionally, until browned.

Add next 5 ingredients. Stir. Reduce heat to medium. Boil gently, uncovered, for about 15 minutes, stirring occasionally, until sauce is thickened and chicken is no longer pink inside.

Sprinkle with cilantro. Makes about 4 cups (1 L).

1 cup (250 mL): 468 Calories; 25.4 g Total Fat (2.3 g Mono, 1.3 g Poly, 19.6 g Sat);
99 mg Cholesterol; 21 g Carbohydrate; 2 g Fibre; 42 g Protein; 265 mg Sodium

Pictured on page 143.

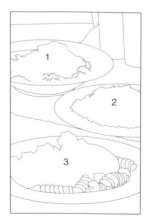

1. Chicken Ratatouille, page 113
2. Chicken And Apricot Pilaf, page 128
3. Chicken And Olives, page 116

Props courtesy of: Dansk Gifts

Chicken Adobo

Adobo a-go-go! Get your groove on with this Filipino favourite.

Coarsely chopped onion	1 1/2 cups	375 mL
Water	1 cup	250 mL
Rice vinegar	1/2 cup	125 mL
Ketchup	3 tbsp.	50 mL
Soy sauce	3 tbsp.	50 mL
Garlic cloves, minced	3	3
Bay leaves	2	2
Sesame oil (for flavour)	1 tsp.	5 mL
Whole cloves	3	3
Dried crushed chilies	1/4 tsp.	1 mL
Chicken legs, back attached (11 – 12 oz., 310 – 340 g, each), skin removed	4	4
Water	1/4 cup	60 mL
Cornstarch	2 tbsp.	30 mL
Sesame seeds, toasted (see Tip, page 13)	2 tsp.	10 mL

Combine first 10 ingredients in Dutch oven or large pot. Bring to a boil on medium. Reduce heat to medium-low.

Add chicken. Simmer, covered, for about 45 minutes, turning chicken at halftime, until chicken is tender. Transfer chicken with slotted spoon to serving platter. Cover to keep warm. Discard bay leaves and cloves. Carefully process sauce with hand blender or in blender until smooth.

Stir water into cornstarch in small cup. Add to sauce. Heat and stir on medium for about 2 minutes until boiling and thickened. Pour over chicken.

Sprinkle with sesame seeds. Serves 4.

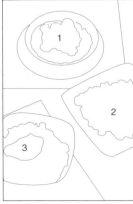

1 serving: 554 Calories; 21.1 g Total Fat (6.0 g Mono, 6.6 g Poly, 4.9 g Sat); 245 mg Cholesterol; 29 g Carbohydrate; 8 g Fibre; 66 g Protein; 1387 mg Sodium

1. Ginger Pineapple Meatballs, page 102
2. Cashew Chicken, page 110
3. Hoisin Chicken Pot, page 120

Props courtesy of: Corelle
                    Cherison Enterprises Inc.

Chicken And Apricot Pilaf

Spend an Arabian night supping on this appetizing dish with real Mid-East flair. The fragrant spices and sweet dried fruit are guaranteed to woo you in at least 1,001 ways!

Cooking oil	1 tbsp.	15 mL
Lean ground chicken	1 lb.	454 g
Chopped onion	1 cup	250 mL
Cinnamon stick (4 inches, 10 cm), see Note	1	1
Whole green cardamom, bruised (see Tip, page 129), see Note	2	2
Curry powder	1 tbsp.	15 mL
Prepared chicken broth	1 3/4 cups	425 mL
Converted white rice	1 cup	250 mL
Chopped dried apricot	1/3 cup	75 mL
Dark raisins	1/3 cup	75 mL
Salt	1/4 tsp.	1 mL
Frozen peas, thawed	2/3 cup	150 mL
Slivered almonds, toasted (see Tip, page 13)	1/3 cup	75 mL
Chopped fresh mint (or 2 tsp., 10 mL, dried)	2 1/2 tbsp.	37 mL

Heat cooking oil in large saucepan on medium-high. Add chicken and onion. Scramble-fry for about 10 minutes until chicken is no longer pink and onion is softened. Drain.

Add next 3 ingredients. Heat and stir for about 1 minute until fragrant.

Add next 5 ingredients. Stir. Bring to a boil. Reduce heat to medium-low. Simmer, covered, for about 15 minutes, without stirring, until rice is tender. Discard cinnamon stick and cardamom.

Add remaining 3 ingredients. Stir. Let stand, covered, for about 5 minutes until heated through. Makes about 6 cups (1.5 L).

1 cup (250 mL): 5408 Calories; 15.3 g Total Fat (2.8 g Mono, 1.3 g Poly, 0.6 g Sat); 0 mg Cholesterol; 47 g Carbohydrate; 4 g Fibre; 21 g Protein; 379 mg Sodium

Pictured on page 125.

Note: If you don't have any cinnamon sticks or cardamom pods on hand, you can use 1/4 tsp. (1 mL) each of ground cinnamon and ground cardamom instead.

Chicken Stroganoff

Everybody will "Russian" to the kitchen to get a whiff of this delicious, creamy chicken dish literally made for royalty. It is purported that the dish was named after Count Stroganov, a member of a very wealthy, well-known Russian family. Great served over egg noodles.

All-purpose flour	1/4 cup	60 mL
Paprika	1/2 tsp.	2 mL
Salt	1/2 tsp.	2 mL
Pepper	1/2 tsp.	2 mL
Boneless, skinless chicken thighs, cut into short strips	1 lb.	454 g
Cooking oil	2 tbsp.	30 mL
Sliced fresh white mushrooms	2 cups	500 mL
Chopped onion	1 1/2 cups	375 mL
Prepared chicken broth	1 cup	250 mL
Dry sherry	3 tbsp.	50 mL
Dijon mustard	1 tsp.	5 mL
Soy sauce	1 tsp.	5 mL
Sour cream	1/2 cup	125 mL
Dried dillweed	1/2 tsp.	2 mL

Combine first 4 ingredients in large resealable freezer bag. Add chicken. Toss until coated. Remove chicken. Discard any remaining flour mixture.

Heat cooking oil in Dutch oven or large pot on medium-high. Add chicken. Cook, uncovered, for about 5 minutes, stirring occasionally, until chicken is browned. Add mushrooms and onion. Cook for 5 to 10 minutes, stirring often, until onion is softened.

Add next 4 ingredients. Heat and stir for 5 minutes, scraping any brown bits from bottom of pan. Reduce heat to medium-low. Simmer, partially covered, for about 10 minutes, stirring occasionally, until thickened.

Add sour cream and dill. Stir. Makes about 4 cups (1 L).

1 cup (250 mL): 358 Calories; 20.9 g Total Fat (7.4 g Mono, 4.2 g Poly, 6.5 g Sat); 94 mg Cholesterol; 14 g Carbohydrate; 1 g Fibre; 25 g Protein; 582 mg Sodium

 tip To bruise cardamom, pound pods with mallet or press with flat side of wide knife to "bruise," or crack them open slightly.

Spinach Chicken Skillet

The well-blended flavours of chicken, nutmeg and dill just seem
to pop when sprinkled with lemon—it's a whole new taste sensation!
This dish requires a large frying-pan with a lid, so if yours doesn't
have one, try the lid from your Dutch oven or wok.

Olive (or cooking) oil	1 tbsp.	15 mL
Boneless, skinless chicken breast halves, cut into 1 inch (2.5 cm) cubes	1 lb.	454 g
Salt	1/2 tsp.	2 mL
Pepper	1/4 tsp.	1 mL
Chopped onion	2 cups	500 mL
Grated lemon zest	2 tsp.	10 mL
Prepared chicken broth	3 cups	750 mL
Converted white rice	1 1/2 cups	375 mL
Ground nutmeg	1/4 tsp.	1 mL
Coarsely chopped fresh spinach leaves, lightly packed	2 cups	500 mL
Chopped fresh dill (or 1 1/2 tsp., 7 mL, dried)	2 tbsp.	30 mL
Lemon juice	1 – 2 tbsp.	15 – 30 mL

Heat olive oil in large frying pan on medium-high. Add chicken. Sprinkle with salt and pepper. Cook for about 5 minutes, stirring occasionally, until starting to brown.

Add onion and lemon zest. Cook for about 5 minutes, stirring often, until onion starts to soften.

Add next 3 ingredients. Stir. Bring to a boil. Reduce heat to medium-low. Simmer, covered, for 20 minutes, without stirring. Remove from heat.

Add spinach and dill. Stir. Let stand, covered, for about 10 minutes until liquid is absorbed and rice is tender.

Add lemon juice. Stir. Makes about 8 cups (2 L).

1 cup (250 mL): 267 Calories; 3.7 g Total Fat (1.8 g Mono, 0.6 g Poly, 0.7 g Sat); 33 mg Cholesterol; 38 g Carbohydrate; 2 g Fibre; 19 g Protein; 456 mg Sodium

Chicken Meatball Sauce

This isn't your kids' spaghetti sauce and meatballs! Rekindle your old childhood romance with the sophisticated flavours of this stylish cinnamon, nutmeg and balsamic vinegar sauce that's all grown up.

Large egg, fork-beaten	1	1
Fine dry bread crumbs	1/2 cup	125 mL
Parsley flakes	1 tsp.	5 mL
Dried oregano	1/2 tsp.	2 mL
Lean ground chicken	1 lb.	454 g
Olive (or cooking) oil	1 tbsp.	15 mL
Chopped onion	1/2 cup	125 mL
Grated carrot	1/2 cup	125 mL
Garlic cloves, minced (or 1/2 tsp., 2 mL, powder)	2	2
Can of diced tomatoes (with juice)	28 oz.	796 mL
Can of tomato sauce	7 1/2 oz.	213 mL
Balsamic vinegar	1/4 cup	60 mL
Granulated sugar	2 tsp.	10 mL
Ground cinnamon	1/2 tsp.	2 mL
Ground nutmeg	1/2 tsp.	2 mL
Pepper	1/4 tsp.	1 mL
Bay leaves	2	2

Combine first 4 ingredients in large bowl.

Add chicken. Mix well. Roll into 1 inch (2.5 cm) balls.

Heat olive oil in large frying pan on medium-high. Add meatballs. Cook for about 5 minutes, turning often, until well browned. Transfer with slotted spoon to paper towel-lined plate to drain. Makes about 35 meatballs.

Add next 3 ingredients to same frying pan. Cook on medium for 3 to 5 minutes, stirring often, until onion starts to soften. Add meatballs.

Process next 7 ingredients in blender until smooth. Add to meatball mixture. Add bay leaves. Stir. Bring to a boil. Reduce heat to medium-low. Simmer, uncovered, for 20 to 25 minutes, stirring occasionally, until sauce is thickened and internal temperature of chicken reaches 175°F (80°C). Discard bay leaves. Makes about 6 cups (1.5 L).

1 cup (250 mL): 262 Calories; 13.9 g Total Fat (2.2 g Mono, 0.4 g Poly, 0.7 g Sat); 31 mg Cholesterol; 18 g Carbohydrate; 1 g Fibre; 17 g Protein; 506 mg Sodium

Chicken And Apple Curry

We know that apples have often been seen as a symbol
of temptation, but serve them with sweet mango and crunchy
pistachios in a creamy curry and they're pretty near irresistible!

Cooking oil	1 tbsp.	15 mL
Boneless, skinless chicken thighs, cut into 1 inch (2.5 cm) cubes	1 lb.	454 g
Sliced fresh white mushrooms	2 cups	500 mL
Chopped onion	1 cup	250 mL
All-purpose flour	2 tbsp.	30 mL
Curry powder	2 tsp.	10 mL
Prepared chicken broth	1 1/2 cups	375 mL
Chopped peeled cooking apple (such as McIntosh)	1 1/2 cups	375 mL
Mango chutney, larger pieces chopped	1/4 cup	60 mL
Chopped pistachios, toasted (see Tip, page 13)	1/2 cup	125 mL
Plain yogurt	1/4 cup	60 mL
Chopped fresh cilantro or parsley	2 tbsp.	30 mL

Heat cooking oil in large saucepan on medium-high. Add chicken. Cook, uncovered, for about 5 minutes, stirring often, until browned.

Add mushrooms and onion. Cook for about 5 minutes, stirring often, until onion is softened.

Sprinkle with flour and curry powder. Heat and stir for 1 minute.

Slowly stir in broth. Bring to a boil, stirring constantly and scraping any brown bits from bottom of pan until thickened.

Add apple and chutney. Stir. Reduce heat to medium-low. Simmer, uncovered, for about 10 minutes, stirring occasionally, until apple is tender.

Add remaining 3 ingredients. Stir. Makes about 4 1/2 cups (1.1 L).

1 cup (250 mL): 353 Calories; 18.4 g Total Fat (8.5 g Mono, 4.8 g Poly, 3.6 g Sat);
68 mg Cholesterol; 23 g Carbohydrate; 3 g Fibre; 25 g Protein; 335 mg Sodium

"Osso Buco" Chicken

No bones about it, this chicken version of osso bucco is delightful.

All-purpose flour	1/4 cup	60 mL
Seasoned salt	1/2 tsp.	2 mL
Bone-in chicken thighs, skin removed (5 – 6 oz., 140 – 170 g, each)	8	8
Cooking oil	2 tbsp.	30 mL
Chopped onion	2 cups	500 mL
Chopped carrot	1 cup	250 mL
Garlic clove, minced (or 1/4 tsp., 1 mL, powder)	1	1
Dried sage	1 tsp.	5 mL
Can of Italian-style stewed tomatoes	19 oz.	540 mL
Can of condensed chicken broth	10 oz.	284 mL
Dry (or alcohol-free) white wine	1 cup	250 mL
Bay leaf	1	1
Chopped fresh parsley	1/4 cup	60 mL
Grated lemon zest	1 tbsp.	15 mL

Combine flour and seasoned salt in large resealable freezer bag. Add chicken. Toss until coated. Remove chicken. Discard any remaining flour mixture.

Heat cooking oil in large frying pan on medium-high. Arrange chicken in pan, spaced apart. Cook for about 5 minutes, turning at halftime, until browned on both sides. Remove to plate. Set aside. Reduce heat to medium.

Add next 4 ingredients to same frying pan. Cook for about 5 minutes, stirring occasionally, until carrot starts to soften.

Add next 4 ingredients. Stir. Bring to a boil, scraping any brown bits from bottom of pan. Add chicken. Reduce heat to medium-low. Simmer, covered, for about 1 hour, stirring occasionally, until chicken is tender. Remove chicken to serving bowl using slotted spoon. Cover to keep warm. Cook sauce, uncovered, on medium for about 10 minutes until thickened. Discard bay leaf. Pour sauce mixture over chicken.

Combine parsley and lemon zest in small cup. Sprinkle over chicken and sauce before serving. Serves 4.

1 serving: 539 Calories; 23.9 g Total Fat (10.5 g Mono, 5.9 g Poly, 5.2 g Sat); 143 mg Cholesterol; 26 g Carbohydrate; 2 g Fibre; 43 g Protein; 799 mg Sodium

Pictured on page 143.

Spinach Orzo Salad

The complaints about eating leftover turkey will soon cease when your friends and family taste this light and fresh salad. This colourful spinach creation contains orzo, a tiny pasta similar in shape to rice.

Water	2 cups	500 mL
Salt	1/4 tsp.	1 mL
Orzo	1/2 cup	125 mL
Fresh spinach leaves, lightly packed	4 cups	1 L
Chopped cooked turkey (see Tip, page 135)	2 cups	500 mL
Diced fresh tomato	1 1/2 cups	375 mL
Kalamata olives, chopped	1/2 cup	125 mL
FETA DRESSING		
Crumbled feta cheese	1/3 cup	75 mL
Olive (or cooking) oil	1/4 cup	60 mL
Balsamic vinegar	2 tbsp.	30 mL
Lemon juice	1 tbsp.	15 mL
Chopped fresh oregano (or 1/4 tsp., 1 mL, dried)	1 tsp.	5 mL
Salt	1/4 tsp.	1 mL
Pepper	1 tsp.	5 mL

Combine water and salt in small saucepan. Bring to a boil. Add orzo. Boil, uncovered, for about 8 minutes, stirring occasionally, until tender but firm. Drain. Rinse with cold water. Drain well. Transfer to large bowl.

Add next 4 ingredients. Toss.

Feta Dressing: Process all 7 ingredients in blender until smooth. Makes about 1/2 cup (125 mL) dressing. Drizzle over salad. Toss. Makes about 8 1/2 cups (2.1 L).

1 cup (250 mL): 210 Calories; 11.4 g Total Fat (7.2 g Mono, 1.2 g Poly, 2.4 g Sat); 37 mg Cholesterol; 14 g Carbohydrate; 1 g Fibre; 13 g Protein; 333 mg Sodium

Pictured on page 144.

Ginger Meatballs

Turkey meatballs! Who would have thought? Well, we did, of course!
These tasty little meatballs are great over rice for dinner
or served with wooden picks as cocktail-party fare.

Large egg, fork-beaten	1	1
Fine dry bread crumbs	1/2 cup	125 mL
Finely chopped pickled ginger slices	3 tbsp.	50 mL
Finely chopped canned water chestnuts	2 tbsp.	30 mL
Finely chopped green onion	2 tbsp.	30 mL
Sweet-and-sour sauce	2 tbsp.	30 mL
Soy sauce	1 tbsp.	15 mL
Salt	1/4 tsp.	1 mL
Extra-lean ground turkey	1 lb.	454 g
Sweet-and-sour sauce	1/2 cup	125 mL

Combine first 8 ingredients in large bowl. Add turkey. Mix well. Roll into
1 1/2 inch (3.8 cm) balls. Arrange on greased baking sheet with sides. Bake
in 400°F (205°C) oven for about 20 minutes until fully cooked and internal
temperature reaches 175°F (80°C).

Heat second amount of sweet-and-sour sauce in medium saucepan on
medium. Add meatballs. Stir gently until coated. Makes about 22 meatballs.

1 meatball: 44 Calories; 0.6 g Total Fat (0.2 g Mono, 0.1 g Poly, 0.1 g Sat); 17 mg Cholesterol;
4 g Carbohydrate; trace Fibre; 6 g Protein; 171 mg Sodium

 tip Don't have any leftover turkey? Start with about 10 oz. (285 g)
boneless, skinless turkey. Place in large frying pan with 1 cup (250 mL)
water or chicken broth. Simmer, covered, for 12 to 14 minutes until
no longer pink inside. Drain. Chop. Makes about 2 cups (500 mL) of
cooked turkey.

Turkey Goat-Cheese Spirals

Put a whole new spin on dinner with these attractive turkey pinwheels. Make them early in the day and serve as appetizers at your next dinner party.

Coarsely chopped fresh basil	1/2 cup	125 mL
Goat (chèvre) cheese	3 oz.	85 g
Sun-dried tomato pesto	1/4 cup	60 mL
Turkey scallopini (about 1 lb., 454 g)	4	4
Thin deli ham slices (about 3 oz., 85 g)	4 – 6	4 – 6
Balsamic vinegar	1 tbsp.	15 mL
Olive oil	1 tbsp.	15 mL

Combine first 3 ingredients in small bowl.

Spread pesto mixture evenly over turkey. Arrange ham slices over pesto, trimming to fit if necessary. Roll up tightly, jelly-roll style. Arrange, seam-side down, on greased baking sheet with sides.

Combine vinegar and olive oil in small cup. Brush over rolls. Bake in 350°F (175°C) oven for about 25 minutes until internal temperature reaches 170°F (77°C). Let stand for about 30 minutes until cool. Wrap in plastic wrap. Chill for at least 4 hours or overnight. Cut each roll into 1/2 inch 12 mm) slices. Makes about 24 spirals.

1 spiral: 47 Calories; 2.0 g Total Fat (0.9 g Mono, 0.2 g Poly, 0.7 g Sat); 15 mg Cholesterol; 1 g Carbohydrate; trace Fibre; 6 g Protein; 81 mg Sodium

Paré Pointer

There's a good reason they all adore their boss.
They'll be fired if they don't.

Turkey

Hot And Sour Turkey Pot Soup

Chicken soup may have the cure-all market cornered, but turkey may just have something to say about that! Familiar and comforting with just the right blend of spicy and sour ingredients, this slow cooker soup will have you on your feet in no time.

Chinese dried mushrooms	6	6
Boiling water	1 cup	250 mL
Prepared chicken broth	4 cups	1 L
Diced cooked turkey (see Tip, page 135)	2 cups	500 mL
Sliced carrot	2 cups	500 mL
Cubed firm tofu	1 cup	250 mL
Sliced celery	1 cup	250 mL
Soy sauce	1/4 cup	60 mL
Rice vinegar	2 tbsp.	30 mL
Chili paste (sambal oelek)	1 tsp.	5 mL
Prepared chicken broth	1/4 cup	60 mL
Cornstarch	2 tbsp.	30 mL
Sesame oil (optional)	1 tsp.	5 mL
Chopped baby bok choy	2 cups	500 mL
Thinly sliced green onion	1/4 cup	60 mL
Rice vinegar	1 tbsp.	15 mL

Put mushrooms into small heatproof bowl. Add boiling water. Stir. Let stand for about 20 minutes until softened. Drain. Remove and discard stems. Slice into thin strips. Transfer to 3 1/2 to 4 quart (3.5 to 4 L) slow cooker.

Add next 8 ingredients. Stir well. Cook, covered, on Low for 4 to 6 hours or High for 2 to 3 hours until carrot is tender.

Combine next 3 ingredients in small bowl. Add to slow cooker. Stir. Add bok choy and green onion. Stir well. Cook, covered, on High for about 5 minutes until slightly thickened.

Stir in second amount of vinegar. Makes about 8 cups (2 L).

1 cup (250 mL): 118 Calories; 2.1 g Total Fat (0.6 g Mono, 0.6 g Poly, 0.6 g Sat); 34 mg Cholesterol; 9 g Carbohydrate; 2 g Fibre; 15 g Protein; 1142 mg Sodium

Smoky Pea Soup

This soup is a real wing-dinger! Smoked turkey wings add
a unique smoky flavour to this pea soup with a twist.

Cooking oil	2 tsp.	10 mL
Chopped onion	3/4 cup	175 mL
Chopped carrot	1/2 cup	125 mL
Chopped celery	1/2 cup	125 mL
Water	8 cups	2 L
Smoked turkey wings	2	2
Green split peas, rinsed and drained	2 cups	500 mL
Diced peeled potato	1 1/2 cups	375 mL
Chicken bouillon cubes (1/5 oz., 6 g, each)	3	3
Bay leaf	1	1
Dried marjoram	1 tsp.	5 mL
Salt	1 tsp.	5 mL
Pepper	1/2 tsp.	2 mL
Dried thyme	1/2 tsp.	2 mL
Ground cloves	1/4 tsp.	1 mL
Lemon juice	2 tbsp.	30 mL

Heat cooking oil in Dutch oven or large pot on medium. Add next
3 ingredients. Cook, uncovered, for 5 to 10 minutes, stirring occasionally,
until vegetables are softened.

Add next 11 ingredients. Stir. Bring to a boil. Reduce heat to medium-low.
Simmer, partially covered, for about 1 1/2 hours, stirring occasionally,
until peas are soft and breaking up (see Note). Remove turkey to cutting
board using tongs. Remove turkey from larger two sections of wings.
Chop turkey. Discard tips, skin and bones. Add turkey to soup. Stir.
Discard bay leaf.

Add lemon juice. Stir. Makes about 9 cups (2.25 L).

1 cup (250 mL): 280 Calories; 12.6 g Total Fat (4.9 g Mono, 3.1 g Poly, 3.2 g Sat);
74.3 mg Cholesterol; 13 g Carbohydrate; 3 g Fibre; 28 g Protein; 1664 mg Sodium

Note: If soup is becoming too thick, add 1 cup (250 mL) water.

Turkey Tetrazzini

This creamy pasta dish is guaranteed to warm you, heart and soul! For those who like to get their warmth from spicy heat, double the amount of cayenne.

Butter (or hard margarine)	1/4 cup	60 mL
Thinly sliced fresh white mushrooms	3 cups	750 mL
All-purpose flour	3 tbsp.	50 mL
Cans of condensed chicken broth (10 oz., 284 mL, each)	2	2
Half-and-half cream	3/4 cup	175 mL
Dry sherry	3 tbsp.	50 mL
Garlic powder	1/4 tsp.	1 mL
Cayenne pepper	1/8 tsp.	0.5 mL
Water	8 cups	2 L
Salt	1 tsp.	5 mL
Spaghetti, broken in half	8 oz.	225 g
Chopped cooked turkey (see Tip, page 135)	2 cups	500 mL
Grated Parmesan cheese	1/3 cup	75 mL
Chopped fresh parsley	1 tbsp.	15 mL

Melt butter in large frying pan on medium. Add mushrooms. Cook for about 10 minutes, stirring occasionally, until mushrooms are golden brown and liquid is evaporated.

Sprinkle with flour. Heat and stir for 1 minute.

Slowly add broth, stirring constantly, until boiling and thickened. Add next 4 ingredients. Cook and stir until heated through. Set aside.

Combine water and salt in Dutch oven or large pot. Bring to a boil. Add spaghetti. Boil, uncovered, for 8 to 10 minutes, stirring occasionally, until tender but firm. Drain. Return to same pot. Add half of mushroom mixture. Stir well. Transfer to greased 2 quart (2 L) shallow baking dish. Make a well in centre.

Add turkey to remaining mushroom mixture. Stir. Add to well.

Sprinkle cheese over top. Bake, uncovered, in 350°F (175°C) oven for about 45 minutes until golden and bubbling.

Sprinkle with parsley. Serve immediately. Serves 4.

1 serving: 602 Calories; 24 g Total Fat (6.4 g Mono, 2.1 g Poly, 13 g Sat); 123 mg Cholesterol; 52 g Carbohydrate; 3.2 g Fibre; 42 g Protein; 1186 mg Sodium

Roasted Brined Turkey

Brine's the way for a magnificently moist turkey (beware of making gravy with the drippings—it will be very salty).

BRINING SOLUTION

Water	2 gallons	8 L
Coarse salt	2 cups	500 mL
Brown sugar, packed	1 1/2 cups	375 mL
Dried thyme	1/4 cup	60 mL
Bay leaves	6	6
Garlic cloves, halved	6	6
Black peppercorns	1 tbsp.	15 mL
Whole turkey, giblets and neck removed (not self-basting)	14 lbs.	6.5 kg
Cooking oil	2 tbsp.	30 mL

Brining Solution: Put first 7 ingredients into extra large container (see Note 1). Stir until salt and sugar are dissolved.

Submerge turkey in brining solution. Let stand, covered, in refrigerator for 12 to 24 hours. Remove turkey from brining solution. Rinse inside and out under running water. Drain. Pat dry with paper towels. Transfer to large roasting pan. Tie wings with butcher's string close to body. Tie legs to tail.

Rub cooking oil over surface of turkey. Bake, uncovered, in 400°F (205°C) oven for 45 minutes. Reduce heat to 325°F (160°C). Bake for about 75 minutes, basting occasionally with pan juices (see Note 2), until meat thermometer inserted in thickest part of thigh reads 165°F (74°C). Remove turkey from oven. Cover with foil. Let stand for 15 minutes before carving. Serves 16.

1 serving: 653 Calories; 33.5 g Total Fat (12.5 g Mono, 8.4 g Poly, 9.1 g Sat); 270 mg Cholesterol; 1 g Carbohydrate; 0 g Fibre; 81 g Protein; 843 mg Sodium

Note 1: Use a non-corrosive container about 5 gallons (20 L) in volume. It must be large enough to hold the turkey completely submerged in the brining solution and must also fit into the refrigerator. A very large stainless steel or enamel stockpot will work fine. Deli or wine brewing stores also sell large food-safe plastic pails. If there is no space in the refrigerator, use a picnic cooler insulated with ice packs to keep the container chilled during the brining process.

Note 2: If the turkey is browning too much or too quickly while roasting, cover with foil.

Maple Glazed Turkey

Traditional flavours meet modern convenience. Enjoy roast turkey and cranberries without having to cook a whole bird.

Boneless, skinless turkey breast half (about 1 1/2 lbs., 680 g)	1	1
Maple (or maple-flavoured) syrup	1/3 cup	75 mL
Salt	1/4 tsp.	1 mL
Pepper	1/4 tsp.	1 mL
Medium oranges, sliced	2	2
ORANGE CRANBERRY COMPOTE		
Brown sugar, packed	1/3 cup	75 mL
Balsamic vinegar	1 tbsp.	15 mL
Fresh (or frozen) cranberries	1 cup	250 mL
Orange juice	3/4 cup	175 mL
Grated orange zest	1 tsp.	5 mL
Star anise	2	2

Place turkey in greased foil-lined 9 × 9 inch (22 × 22 cm) baking dish. Brush with half of syrup. Sprinkle with salt and pepper. Arrange orange slices over turkey. Bake in 400°F (205°C) oven for 30 minutes. Remove and discard orange slices. Brush with syrup. Bake for another 15 minutes, brushing with syrup every 5 minutes, until browned and internal temperature reaches 170°F (77°C). Cover with foil. Let stand for 10 minutes. Cut turkey crosswise into 1/4 inch (6 mm) slices.

Orange Cranberry Compote: Combine brown sugar and vinegar in small saucepan. Heat and stir on medium until brown sugar is dissolved.

Add remaining 4 ingredients. Stir. Bring to a boil. Reduce heat to medium-low. Simmer, uncovered, for about 10 minutes until cranberries split and sauce is thickened. Remove from heat. Discard anise. Makes about 1 cup (250 mL) compote. Serve with turkey. Serves 6.

1 serving: 236 Calories; 2.2 g Total Fat (0.9 g Mono, 0.5 g Poly, 0.7 g Sat); 58 mg Cholesterol; 28 g Carbohydrate; 1 g Fibre; 26 g Protein; 181 mg Sodium

Pulled Tex Turkey

Got a hankerin' for some good, old southwestern sandwich flavour?
Then, yee doggies, this is the meal for you! Sweet and tangy
with an authentic flavour. Don't forget the napkins!

Sliced onion	1 1/2 cups	375 mL
Barbecue sauce	1 cup	250 mL
Can of tomato sauce	7 1/2 oz.	213 mL
Can of diced green chilies	4 oz.	113 g
Chili powder	1 tbsp.	15 mL
Dried oregano	1 tsp.	5 mL
Ground cumin	1/2 tsp.	2 mL
Ground cinnamon	1/4 tsp.	1 mL
Boneless, skinless turkey thighs	1 3/4 lbs.	790 g
Kaiser rolls, split	6	6

Combine first 8 ingredients in 3 1/2 to 4 quart (3.5 to 4 L) slow cooker. Add turkey. Spoon barbecue sauce mixture over turkey to cover. Cook, covered, on Low for 7 to 8 hours or on High for 3 1/2 to 4 hours until turkey is tender. Remove turkey to cutting board using tongs. Shred turkey using 2 forks. Add to sauce mixture. Stir.

Serve turkey mixture in rolls. Makes 6 sandwiches.

1 sandwich: 400 Calories; 10.6 g Total Fat (3.7 g Mono, 2.9 g Poly, 2.5 g Sat); 111 mg Cholesterol; 43 g Carbohydrate; 4 g Fibre; 33 g Protein; 1059 mg Sodium

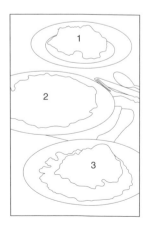

1. "Osso Bucco" Chicken, page 133
2. Black Bean Chili, page 115
3. Pineapple Chicken Bliss, page 124

Props courtesy of: Dansk Gifts
Pier 1 Imports

Sesame Turkey Cutlets

Cutlets are no longer blah when you add some Asian flair! Sesame, ginger and soy sauce add character to this pan-fried favourite.

Large egg	1	1
Soy sauce	1 tbsp.	15 mL
Fine dry bread crumbs	1/2 cup	125 mL
Sesame seeds	1/4 cup	60 mL
Salt	1 tsp.	5 mL
Pepper	1/2 tsp.	2 mL
Ground ginger	1/4 tsp.	1 mL
Turkey breast cutlets (about 4 oz., 113 g, each)	4	4
Cooking oil	3 tbsp.	50 mL

Beat egg and soy sauce with fork in small shallow dish.

Combine next 5 ingredients in separate small shallow dish.

Dip cutlets into egg mixture. Press both sides of cutlets into crumb mixture until coated. Discard any remaining egg and crumb mixture.

Heat cooking oil in large frying pan on medium. Add cutlets. Cook for 3 to 4 minutes per side until golden and no longer pink inside. Makes 4 cutlets.

1 cutlet: 314 Calories; 17.2 g Total Fat (8.9 g Mono, 5.3 g Poly, 2.3 g Sat); 93 mg Cholesterol; 10 g Carbohydrate; 1 g Fibre; 29 g Protein; 887 mg Sodium

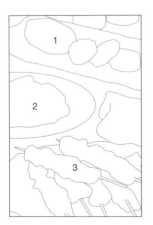

1. Sun-Dried Tomato Turkey Roll, page 148
2. Spinach Orzo Salad, page 134
3. Spice Cupboard Kabobs, page 146

Props courtesy of: Cherison Enterprises Inc.

Spice Cupboard Kabobs

Pay attention to your neglected spices and put them to work in these tandoori-style kabobs. Factor the long marinating time into your planning.

Plain yogurt	3/4 cup	175 mL
Finely chopped onion (or 1 tbsp., 15 mL, flakes)	1/4 cup	60 mL
Lemon juice	3 tbsp.	50 mL
Garlic cloves, minced (or 3/4 tsp., 4 mL, powder)	3	3
All-purpose flour	1 tbsp.	15 mL
Finely grated gingerroot (or 1/2 tsp., 2 mL, ground ginger)	2 tsp.	10 mL
Cayenne pepper	1 tsp.	5 mL
Dry mustard	1 tsp.	5 mL
Ground coriander	1 tsp.	5 mL
Ground cumin	1 tsp.	5 mL
Paprika	1 tsp.	5 mL
Ground cinnamon	1/4 tsp.	1 mL
Turmeric	1/4 tsp.	1 mL
Ground cardamom	1/8 tsp.	0.5 mL
Boneless, skinless turkey breast half (about 1 1/2 lbs, 680 g), cut into 1 inch (2.5 cm) cubes	1	1
Bamboo skewers (8 inches, 20 cm, each), soaked in water for 10 minutes	12	12
Salt	1/4 tsp.	1 mL
Chopped fresh cilantro or parsley	1 tbsp.	15 mL

Combine first 14 ingredients in small bowl.

Put turkey into large resealable freezer bag. Add yogurt mixture. Seal bag. Turn until coated. Let stand in refrigerator for at least 6 hours or overnight, turning occasionally. Remove turkey. Discard any remaining yogurt mixture.

Thread turkey onto skewers. Sprinkle with salt. Preheat gas barbecue to medium (see Tip, page 21). Cook kabobs on greased grill for 12 to 14 minutes, turning occasionally, until no longer pink inside. Remove to serving platter.

(continued on next page)

Turkey

Sprinkle with cilantro. Makes 12 kabobs.

1 kabob: 72 Calories; 0.7 g Total Fat (0.1 g Mono, 0.1 g Poly, 0.3 g Sat); 36 mg Cholesterol;
1 g Carbohydrate; trace Fibre; 14 g Protein; 81 mg Sodium

Pictured on page 144.

Turkey Parmesan Schnitzel

A simple supper, indeed! Turkey schnitzel is easy to make and sure to please the
entire family. Perfect with a squeeze of fresh lemon and a sprinkle of parsley.

All-purpose flour	1/2 cup	125 mL
Paprika	1 tsp.	5 mL
Seasoned salt	1 tsp.	5 mL
Pepper	1/4 tsp.	1 mL
Large eggs	2	2
Water	1 tbsp.	15 mL
Fine dry bread crumbs	1/2 cup	125 mL
Grated Parmesan cheese	1/2 cup	125 mL
Turkey scallopini (about 1 lb., 454 g)	4	4
Cooking oil	4 tsp.	20 mL
Butter (or hard margarine)	4 tsp.	20 mL
Lemon wedges (optional)	4	4

Combine first 4 ingredients on plate.

Beat eggs and water with fork in small shallow bowl.

Combine bread crumbs and cheese on separate plate.

Press both sides of turkey into flour mixture. Dip into egg mixture. Press both sides of turkey into crumb mixture until coated. Discard any remaining flour, egg and crumb mixture.

Heat 1 tsp. (5 mL) each of cooking oil and butter in large frying pan on medium. Add turkey. Cook, in batches, for about 2 minutes per side, adding cooking oil and butter 1 tsp. (5 mL) each at a time, as required for each batch, until no longer pink inside.

Serve with lemon wedges. Makes 4 schnitzel.

1 schnitzel: 405 Calories; 16.2 g Total Fat (6.3 g Mono, 2.4 g Poly, 6.3 g Sat); 183 mg Cholesterol;
23 g Carbohydrate; 1 g Fibre; 40 g Protein; 812 mg Sodium

Sun-Dried Tomato Turkey Roll

Got an itch that only turkey will scratch but don't feel like cooking up a whole bird? Prepare this attractive turkey roll instead. The colourful filling creates a striking red-orange pinwheel design once the roll is cut into slices.

Boneless, skinless turkey breast half (about 1 1/2 lbs., 680 g)	1	1
Sun-dried tomatoes in oil, blotted dry and chopped	1/2 cup	125 mL
Grated Parmesan cheese	3 tbsp.	50 mL
Olive (or cooking) oil	2 tbsp.	30 mL
Garlic cloves, minced (or 1/2 tsp., 2 mL, powder)	2	2
Chopped fresh rosemary	2 tsp.	10 mL
Dried crushed chilies	1/4 tsp.	1 mL
Salt	1/4 tsp.	1 mL
Pepper	1/2 tsp.	2 mL
Bacon slices	4	4

Sprigs of fresh rosemary, for garnish

To butterfly turkey, cut horizontally lengthwise almost, but not quite through, to other side. Open flat. Place between 2 sheets of plastic wrap. Pound with mallet or rolling pin to 1/2 inch (12 mm) thickness.

Combine next 8 ingredients in small bowl. Spread evenly on cut side of turkey. Roll up tightly, jelly-roll style, starting from long edge. Tie with butcher's string. Place on greased wire rack set in baking sheet with sides or small roasting pan.

Lay bacon slices diagonally over roll. Bake in 350°F (175°C) oven for about 1 1/2 hours until internal temperature reaches 170°F (77°C). Remove to platter. Cover with foil. Let stand for 10 minutes. Remove and discard butcher's string. Cut roll into 3/4 inch (2 cm) slices.

Garnish individual servings with rosemary sprigs. Serves 6.

1 serving: 270 Calories; 15.6 g Total Fat (10.1 g Mono, 2.3 g Poly, 6.0 g Sat); 71 mg Cholesterol; 3 g Carbohydrate; 1 g Fibre; 29 g Protein; 350 mg Sodium

Pictured on page 144.

Boxing Week Turkey Risotto

Forget turkey surprise – this risotto makes leftovers sublime!

Prepared chicken broth	5 cups	1.25 L
Cooking oil	2 tbsp.	30 mL
Chopped onion	1 cup	250 mL
Garlic clove, minced (or 1/4 tsp., 1 mL, powder)	1	1
Mild Italian sausage, casing removed, cut into 1/2 inch (12 mm) pieces	1	1
Bay leaf	1	1
Dried thyme	1/2 tsp.	2 mL
Arborio rice	1 1/4 cups	300 mL
Dry (or alcohol-free) white wine	1/2 cup	125 mL
Chopped cooked turkey (see Tip, page 135)	2 cups	500 mL
Frozen Brussels sprouts, thawed and halved	1 1/2 cups	375 mL
Grated Parmesan cheese	1/3 cup	75 mL
Butter (or hard margarine)	2 tbsp.	30 mL

Measure broth into medium saucepan. Bring to a boil. Reduce heat to low. Cover to keep hot.

Heat cooking oil in large saucepan on medium. Add onion and garlic. Cook, uncovered, for about 2 minutes, stirring often, until onion starts to soften.

Add next 3 ingredients. Scramble-fry (see Note) for 5 to 10 minutes until onion is softened and sausage is no longer pink.

Add rice to sausage mixture. Cook and stir for about 2 minutes until rice is transparent. Add wine. Cook, stirring constantly, until wine is almost absorbed. Add 1 cup (250 mL) hot broth, stirring constantly, until broth is absorbed. Repeat with remaining broth, 1 cup (250 mL) at a time, until broth is absorbed and rice is tender. Entire process will take about 25 minutes. Discard bay leaf.

Add remaining 4 ingredients. Cook and stir for about 2 minutes until heated through. Serve immediately. Makes about 6 cups (1.5 L).

1 cup (250 mL): 359 Calories; 16.7 g Total Fat (6.9 g Mono, 2.7 g Poly, 6.0 g Sat); 73 mg Cholesterol; 21 g Carbohydrate; 2 g Fibre; 26 g Protein; 968 mg Sodium

Note: While stirring be careful not to break up the bay leaf.

Measurement Tables

Throughout this book measurements are given in Conventional and Metric measure. To compensate for differences between the two measurements due to rounding, a full metric measure is not always used. The cup used is the standard 8 fluid ounce. Temperature is given in degrees Fahrenheit and Celsius. Baking pan measurements are in inches and centimetres as well as quarts and litres. An exact metric conversion is given below as well as the working equivalent (Metric Standard Measure).

Spoons

Conventional Measure	Metric Exact Conversion Millilitre (mL)	Metric Standard Measure Millilitre (mL)
1/8 teaspoon (tsp.)	0.6 mL	0.5 mL
1/4 teaspoon (tsp.)	1.2 mL	1 mL
1/2 teaspoon (tsp.)	2.4 mL	2 mL
1 teaspoon (tsp.)	4.7 mL	5 mL
2 teaspoons (tsp.)	9.4 mL	10 mL
1 tablespoon (tbsp.)	14.2 mL	15 mL

Cups

Conventional Measure	Metric Exact Conversion Millilitre (mL)	Metric Standard Measure Millilitre (mL)
1/4 cup (4 tbsp.)	56.8 mL	60 mL
1/3 cup (5 1/3 tbsp.)	75.6 mL	75 mL
1/2 cup (8 tbsp.)	113.7 mL	125 mL
2/3 cup (10 2/3 tbsp.)	151.2 mL	150 mL
3/4 cup (12 tbsp.)	170.5 mL	175 mL
1 cup (16 tbsp.)	227.3 mL	250 mL
4 1/2 cups	1022.9 mL	1000 mL (1 L)

Oven Temperatures

Fahrenheit (°F)	Celsius (°C)
175°	80°
200°	95°
225°	110°
250°	120°
275°	140°
300°	150°
325°	160°
350°	175°
375°	190°
400°	205°
425°	220°
450°	230°
475°	240°
500°	260°

Dry Measurements

Conventional Measure Ounces (oz.)	Metric Exact Conversion Grams (g)	Metric Standard Measure Grams (g)
1 oz.	28.3 g	28 g
2 oz.	56.7 g	57 g
3 oz.	85.0 g	85 g
4 oz.	113.4 g	125 g
5 oz.	141.7 g	140 g
6 oz.	170.1 g	170 g
7 oz.	198.4 g	200 g
8 oz.	226.8 g	250 g
16 oz.	453.6 g	500 g
32 oz.	907.2 g	1000 g (1 kg)

Pans

Conventional Inches	Metric Centimetres
8x8 inch	20x20 cm
9x9 inch	22x22 cm
9x13 inch	22x33 cm
10x15 inch	25x38 cm
11x17 inch	28x43 cm
8x2 inch round	20x5 cm
9x2 inch round	22x5 cm
10x4 1/2 inch tube	25x11 cm
8x4x3 inch loaf	20x10x7.5 cm
9x5x3 inch loaf	22x12.5x7.5 cm

Casseroles

CANADA & BRITAIN		UNITED STATES	
Standard Size Casserole	Exact Metric Measure	Standard Size Casserole	Exact Metric Measure
1 qt. (5 cups)	1.13 L	1 qt. (4 cups)	900 mL
1 1/2 qts. (7 1/2 cups)	1.69 L	1 1/2 qts. (6 cups)	1.35 L
2 qts. (10 cups)	2.25 L	2 qts. (8 cups)	1.8 L
2 1/2 qts. (12 1/2 cups)	2.81 L	2 1/2 qts. (10 cups)	2.25 L
3 qts. (15 cups)	3.38 L	3 qts. (12 cups)	2.7 L
4 qts. (20 cups)	4.5 L	4 qts. (16 cups)	3.6 L
5 qts. (25 cups)	5.63 L	5 qts. (20 cups)	4.5 L

Recipe Index

151

C

D

152

153

M

N

O

P

Q

R

155

T

U

V

W

Z

Company's Coming cookbooks are available at retail locations throughout Canada!

EXCLUSIVE mail order offer on next page

Buy any 2 cookbooks—choose a 3rd FREE of equal or lesser value than the lowest price paid.

Original Series — CA$15.99 Canada — US$12.99 USA & International

CODE		CODE		CODE	
SQ	150 Delicious Squares	CFK	Cook For Kids	WM	30-Minute Weekday Meals
CA	Casseroles	SCH	Stews, Chilies & Chowders	SDL	School Days Lunches
MU	Muffins & More	FD	Fondues	PD	Potluck Dishes
SA	Salads	CCBE	The Beef Book	GBR	Ground Beef Recipes
AP	Appetizers	RC	The Rookie Cook	FRIR	4-Ingredient Recipes
SS	Soups & Sandwiches	RHR	Rush-Hour Recipes	KHC	Kids' Healthy Cooking
CO	Cookies	SW	Sweet Cravings	MM	Mostly Muffins
PA	Pasta	YRG	Year-Round Grilling	SP	Soups
BA	Barbecues	GG	Garden Greens	SU	Simple Suppers
PR	Preserves	CHC	Chinese Cooking	CCDC	Diabetic Cooking
CH	Chicken, Etc.	PK	The Pork Book	CHN	Chicken Now
CT	Cooking For Two	RL	Recipes For Leftovers	KDS	Kids Do Snacks
SC	Slow Cooker Recipes	EB	The Egg Book		*NEW* July 1/07
SF	Stir-Fry	SDPP	School Days Party Pack		
MAM	Make-Ahead Meals	HS	Herbs & Spices		
PB	The Potato Book	BEV	The Beverage Book		
CCLFC	Low-Fat Cooking	SCD	Slow Cooker Dinners		

Cookbook Author Biography

CODE	CA$15.99 Canada US$12.99 USA & International
JP	Jean Paré: An Appetite for Life

Most Loved Recipe Collection

CODE	CA$23.99 Canada US$19.99 USA & International
MLA	Most Loved Appetizers
MLMC	Most Loved Main Courses
MLT	Most Loved Treats
MLBQ	Most Loved Barbecuing
MLCO	Most Loved Cookies

CODE	CA$24.99 Canada US$19.99 USA & International
MLSD	Most Loved Salads & Dressings
MLCA	Most Loved Casseroles
MLSF	Most Loved Stir-Fries

3-in-1 Cookbook Collection

CODE	CA$29.99 Canada US$24.99 USA & International
QEE	Quick & Easy Entertaining
MNT	Meals in No Time

Lifestyle Series

CODE	CA$17.99 Canada US$15.99 USA & International
DC	Diabetic Cooking

CODE	CA$19.99 Canada US$15.99 USA & International
DDI	Diabetic Dinners
LCR	Low-Carb Recipes
HR	Easy Healthy Recipes
HH	Healthy in a Hurry
WGR	Whole Grain Recipes
	NEW August 1/07

Special Occasion Series

CODE	CA$20.99 Canada US$19.99 USA & International
GFK	Gifts from the Kitchen

CODE	CA$24.99 Canada US$19.99 USA & International
BSS	Baking—Simple to Sensational
CGFK	Christmas Gifts from the Kitchen
TR	Timeless Recipes for All Occasions

CODE	CA$27.99 Canada US$22.99 USA & International
CCEL	Christmas Celebrations

Order **ONLINE** for fast delivery!

Log onto **www.companyscoming.com**, browse through our library of cookbooks, gift sets and newest releases and place your order using our fast and secure online order form.

Buy 2, Get 1 FREE!

Buy any 2 cookbooks—choose a **3rd FREE** of equal or lesser value than the lowest price paid.

Title	Code	Quantity	Price	Total
			$	$
DON'T FORGET to indicate your FREE BOOK(S). (see exclusive mail order offer above) please print				

TOTAL BOOKS (including FREE)

TOTAL BOOKS PURCHASED: $

	International	USA	Canada
Shipping & Handling First Book (per destination)	$ 11.98 (one book)	$ 6.98 (one book)	$ 5.98 (one book)
Additional Books (include FREE books)	$ ($4.99 each)	$ ($1.99 each)	$ ($1.99 each)
Sub-Total	$	$	$
Canadian residents add GST/HST			$
TOTAL AMOUNT ENCLOSED	$	$	$

Terms

- All orders must be prepaid. Sorry, no CODs.
- Prices are listed in Canadian Funds for Canadian orders, or US funds for US & International orders.
- Prices are subject to change without prior notice.
- Canadian residents must pay GST/HST (no provincial tax required).
- No tax is required for orders outside Canada.
- Satisfaction is guaranteed or return within 30 days for a full refund.
- Make cheque or money order payable to: **Company's Coming Publishing Limited** 2311-96 Street, Edmonton, Alberta Canada T6N 1G3.
- Orders are shipped surface mail. For courier rates, visit our website: **www.companyscoming.com** or contact us: **Tel: 780-450-6223 Fax: 780-450-1857.**

☐ MasterCard ☐ VISA Expiry ___ / ___ MO/YR

Credit Card # _____

Name of cardholder _____

Cardholder signature _____

Shipping Address Send the cookbooks listed above to:

☐ **Please check if this is a Gift Order**

Name: _____

Street: _____

City: _____ Prov./State: _____

Postal Code/Zip: _____ Country: _____

Tel: (___) _____

E-mail address: _____

Your privacy is important to us. We will not share your e-mail address or personal information with any outside party.

☐ **YES! Please add me to your News Bite e-mail newsletter.**

Gift Giving

- Let us help you with your gift giving!
- We will send cookbooks directly to the recipients of your choice if you give us their names and addresses.
- Please specify the titles you wish to send to each person.
- If you would like to include a personal note or card, we will be pleased to enclose it with your gift order.
- Company's Coming Cookbooks make excellent gifts: birthdays, bridal showers, Mother's Day, Father's Day, graduation or any occasion ...collect them all!

Cookmark

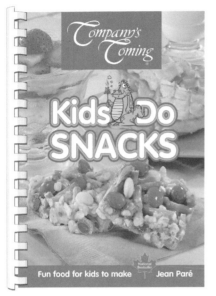

Know a budding chef who's eager to cook? Company's Coming presents *Kids Do Snacks*—a fun cookbook that lets kids become the masters of the kitchen. From *Blend It!* to *Bake It!*, the chapters are arranged so young cooks-in-training can learn more and more tricks and techniques as they go along—making it suitable for kids of all skill levels.

COOKBOOKS

Quick
&
Easy
Recipes

Everyday
Ingredients

Canada's
most popular
cookbooks!